ONE MOVE AT A TIME

ORRIN C. HUDSON

ONE MOVE AT A TIME

HOW TO PLAY AND WIN AT CHESS

...and Life!

10 Finger Press   **Soquel CA**

About the Author

A former Alabama State Trooper, Orrin Hudson won back-to-back victories in the Birmingham City Chess Championships in 1999 and 2000. Soon after, he realized he could teach others how to think strategically, plan effectively and build self confidence – using chess as his vehicle. Focusing his talents on children, he formed Be Someone, (www.besomeone.org,) a non-profit organization through which he and others help children believe in themselves.

Be Someone has helped over 16,000 youth since its inception. Due to this enormous success, Orrin was honored with the National Self Esteem Award and the Black Enterprise Magazine Everyday Hero Award. In addition, he has won a dozen other community service awards from prestigious organizations including the Atlanta Braves, TBS, Harvard University, and the NAACP.

Orrin is married, has four children, and lives in Atlanta, Georgia.

Table of Contents

Foreword

I played one game of chess with Orrin Hudson. He beat me. But I've never had so much fun losing.

He was attending one of my workshops when he challenged me to a friendly contest. Orrin talked fast and played even faster, joking and jiving the whole way. Despite the outward show he put on, it didn't take me long to see that Orrin truly lives within the chessboard. The pieces become his arms and legs, every tactic a step in a carefully considered plan, every move a serious commitment toward winning.

I was no match for him. Our game ended with a lesson: "I won because I sacrificed pieces, Jack," Orrin said with a twinkle in his eye. "You lost because you weren't looking at the big picture."

"The big picture" is at the heart of Orrin's work as a chess instructor. His goal is to do much more than simply give his students the skills they need to be better players. He builds a foundation to make them better people. His work is aimed at anyone and everyone, but he places a special emphasis on bringing direction to those headed down a dark path. Orrin's belief that chess can transform lives has taken him on a mission to save some of the toughest kids in the toughest places, with enormously positive and inspiring results. Because of him these troubled youths are wielding Rooks and Bishops instead of knives and guns.

And if playing chess with Orrin is memorable, watching him with his students is unforgettable. Nobody brings this game to life as vividly as he can; it's a uniquely creative method closer to preaching than teaching. He sings and dances his way through chess lessons in a whirlwind of energy, letting himself go in the joy of the moment. You can't help but be swept up in the experience. The magic he works will soon have even the quietest kid in the room smiling and shouting.

Orrin is a special teacher, and *One Move at a Time* is a special book. You'll learn a lot more than just how to play and win. Within these pages Orrin weaves rules together with ethics, and ties sound strategy to timeless wisdom. The life lessons he offers are powerful tools for developing perspective as a person and a player.

Whether you're a newbie or a chess veteran, this book will help you make the most successful moves you can on the chess board – and even more important—in your life.

I don't know when I'll get to play chess with Orrin again, but now that I've read *One Move at a Time*, I have a much better chance of winning.

Jack Canfield
Co-creator of the *Chicken Soup for the Soul*® series
and author of *The Success Principles*™

Acknowledgements

I owe a tremendous debt of gratitude to several very successful entrepreneurs who have caught my vision and aligned to support my work. Jim Huling, CEO of Matrix Resources, Jane Fonda, TBS- Turner Broadcasting Systems, Steve Harrison of Bradley Communications, Bob Littell of Littell Consulting Services, Joan DuBois of US Chess, John Reese, Armand Morin, Alex Mandossian, and Joe Polish, among others, have generously given of their time, expertise, resources and friendship to keep my work moving forward. These friends never cease to amaze me with their generosity and the depth of their knowledge.

I want to acknowledge the authors, speakers, and publishers, and the folks who work for them, who have given me encouragement and support in my journey: Les Brown, Jack Canfield, John Childress, Vic Conant, Mark Victor Hansen, Keith Harrell, Bob Lane, Mary McKay, Anthony Robbins, Jim Rohn, Brian Tracy, Dottie Walters and Zig Ziglar.

I am thankful for the support and encouragement of my family. Especially my beloved wife Janice, who has been a rock and a shelter when I was tossed upon the sea of doubt, not knowing if I would be able to continue my work. Her belief in me and the countless hours she has spent working closely by my side reflect the love we feel for each other. I also thank my four beautiful children for the lessons they teach me each day: Jordan, Keith, Clairerencia, and Doc.

I am grateful to my mother Margaret Hudson for having 13 children and being there for me.

My high school teacher James Edge mentored me for four years and bought me my first chess book—the only chess book I ever had for many years. Without him I couldn't have ever written this.

I also thank Chris Psaros and Mahesh Grossman of The Authors Team for their help in organizing this book and getting it published.

During the last four years I have made tremendous strides in bringing the principles of my non-profit organization, *Be Someone* to the foreground. It took the help, support and generosity of many people. In particular, Chula Schlesinger has been a wonderful person I could always depend on.

Lastly, I thank God for my life and for placing me in the path of such stellar mentors and caring friends. God has clearly guided my steps to find my dream and has given me the courage and strength to pursue it against all odds, one move at a time.

With love and gratitude,

Orrin C. Hudson
Atlanta, Georgia

PART I

How to Play and Win at Chess

Chapter 1

Say Yes to Chess

Long ago, in a faraway land, there lived a great king. His kingdom was beautiful, vast and full of riches.

But for all of his power and good fortune, the king was afraid.

He knew that there were other kings in other kingdoms who envied what he had, and wanted it all for themselves.

The king worried night and day about what might happen to his land if one of these kings invaded.

He didn't know if he and his army would be prepared to defend themselves. He wanted nothing more than to lay his fears to rest, but he wasn't sure how to do that.

One day the king had an idea.

He went to his most trusted advisers and said, "You are my wisest men. I am not a king who looks for war, but I fear that one day war might come to me. I want you to find a way to keep my mind sharp and alert and prepared for battle, so that I will know how to direct my army if my kingdom falls under siege."

The wise men went off to find a solution for the king.

Weeks later, the king returned to the wise men again and asked, "Have you come up with an answer?"

They showed him a game.

At first, the king was angry. "I will not learn to defend myself playing a game," he said.

But the wise men asked the king to trust them, so he sat down and they taught him how to play. They played many games, over many days, and soon the king understood that the game was exactly what he needed.

The king was impressed. He thanked the wise men, then went off to teach it to his army's generals.

His generals, in turn, taught it to their soldiers.

The soldiers then brought it to the common people.

The new game of "chess" captured the hearts of the entire kingdom. It quickly spread to other kingdoms, and then to other countries.

In time, chess was being played all over the world.

And all the kings, and all their armies, and all the common folk grew stronger and wiser from the lessons they learned playing this simple game.

Why Chess?

Welcome to the game of kings.

In this book, you'll learn how to play chess – the greatest game ever invented. But you won't just learn to play. You'll get all the tools you need to become a successful, winning player

Why should you learn to play chess? The answer is simple. Chess is a great skill builder for life! Start playing and you'll find yourself growing and developing in ways you never imagined.

You will gain:

- Self-confidence
- The ability to set goals and carry them out
- Clearer thinking
- Common sense
- Planning skills

- Concentration

- Patience

And that's just the beginning of a long list! In this book, I'll demonstrate how you can apply your chess skills to your daily life.

Meet Your Teacher

My name is Orrin C. Hudson. For the past 13 years, I've been teaching children how to play chess. I believe every child can be a winner at chess *and* at life. My students have won many championships. Some of my fifth- and sixth-grade students have challenged and beaten college students.

My older brother Eric taught me how to play chess in 1979. I loved the game from the start, and was determined to get better at it. As I improved, I began to beat my brother.

Mr. James Edge, a teacher of mine, saw the potential in me to be a winner. He took me under his wing and helped me improve my game. It was through his encouragement that I became the champion I am today.

As your chess teacher, I will bring out the champion in you.

I have beaten college professors, local chess stars, and won the championship of the Birmingham, Alabama citywide chess tournament, back to back in 1999 and 2000.

Since then, I have interviewed, played and beaten chess masters from all over the world.

Chess is my life. Chess *is* life. And I want to bring it into yours.

My Goal

Several years ago, I started an organization called *Be Someone*. It is my desire to help young people find their inner strengths and inspire them to be the best they can be.

I believe that to *Be Someone* is within reach of any person. Each of us has the seed, but it will grow only if we give it the proper care and water.

Playing chess can be an experience where we learn, live, laugh, love, study, work, play and weep together, while rejoicing through it all. In doing so, we build a vision of the kind of world we want to live in.

Although 26 percent of the world's population is youth, 100 percent of our youth is our future. You are our future, and you hold the key to how successful our society will become.

You don't have to be a young person to learn from this book, though. While I focus most of my teaching on children, this book could be useful to everyone. It's never too late to learn to play chess, or to improve your game.

And just like the king who wanted a solution to his problem – who wanted to strengthen his mind and his abilities – you too can grow through chess and arm yourself with the skills you'll need to live a successful life.

Chess is Easy

You might think chess is a difficult game. You might have seen long, complicated books about it. You might have heard about grand masters going up against sophisticated chess computers.

Don't worry. You don't need to be a genius to play. You'll be surprised to learn that chess is easier than you think.

Yes, there is a lot to learn, and always a deeper level to take your study. But the real beauty of the game is how simple it is to learn the basics.

I once taught a 4-year-old girl to play. She picked it up easily and was beating kids twice her age in no time.

Anyone can learn. And anyone can win, with the right attitude and the right knowledge.

Chess is Cool

On the surface, chess might look boring. It might seem like there's an invisible wall between you and the people who play it. But start playing and you'll see right away how exciting it is.

Chess is a battle – It's a war between two minds!

Chess is a sport – Although chess is not a physical sport, it *is* a sport, nevertheless. It can be as lively and entertaining as any football or basketball game. The excitement stems from its rich strategy, tactics, imagination and human struggle.

Chess is a culture – People react to chess as they do to sports, TV shows and movies. Chess fans follow their favorite teams, discuss players' personalities, argue rules, recite statistics and compare the ratings and rankings of players.

Chess lets you be creative – You will do all sorts of creative things as you seek solutions to chess problems.

Chess is a great way to socialize – It's a friendly, competitive activity, where no one gets hurt. Instead of two bodies slamming into each other (like football), a meeting of two minds takes place. Chess helps develop great social skills. You'll meet a lot of people and make new friends. It gives players and spectators a sense of belonging.

You can play anywhere, anytime – You can play against your family, your friends or in a chess club. You can even play over the Internet or against a computer. You don't need expensive equipment. You don't need to travel to a special place. You don't even need a coach or team.

All you need is a board, chess pieces and an opponent.

Chess Will Help You Succeed in School

The benefits of chess have been scientifically tested and documented. Chess is connected academically, socially and intellectually to a person's development.

In my 25 years of experience with the game, I have witnessed something amazing: Many students who learn to play chess perform better in class.

I have been stunned to see children who had trouble concentrating on a task for more than 20 minutes pick up the game quickly. They were later able to perform a task that lasted up to an hour and a half.

Studies show that there definitely is a connection between playing the game and increased studying skills.

Not only will chess strengthen your character by bestowing you with all sorts of useful life skills, you'll become smarter and more attentive as you learn and improve!

Don't be surprised if your test scores soar as you become a better chess player. In fact, you can expect it.

And even if you already are a strong student, know that every brain needs exercise. Chess is an all-around mental workout!

Chess Opens Your Mind

Chess uses many different parts of your brain to awaken sleeping mental powers.

You could find yourself demonstrating new skills, thinking in different ways and finding better ways to approach problems.

Chess can open the floodgates in your mind and allow power to pour from the well of untapped potential inside you.

I want to take you – a young person of our future, a young person who wants to be someone – and help you discover the scope of your abilities.

What's in This Book?

I will teach you:

- How chess is set up and played
- How to read and record chess games
- Basic strategies and tactics
- How to play through a winning game, step by step, from start to finish.

And in the second part of this book, I will demonstrate 20 different lessons you can learn from playing chess, and how to apply them to your life.

Ready, Set, GO!

Chess has been played all over the world for hundreds of years. It is the most popular board game of all time, with no sign of a slowdown.

Chess is a language all its own. Millions of players worldwide might speak different languages, but they understand each other through the universal language of chess.

You're about to find out why this game is so widespread and why it has lasted so long. Chess is mysterious, deep, calming, exhilarating – even beautiful! And it's a game that anyone can learn. All you need is the *desire* to learn.

So read on and discover the rewards, benefits and many doors that will open as you learn to play chess... one move at a time!

Chapter 2

All the Right Moves

Nobody knows for sure if the story I told you at the beginning of this book is actually true.

Chess is so old, and is played in so many places in the world, that it's difficult to trace its roots. There are many theories, but very few definite answers.

Where and when chess was invented is a mystery.

But most scholars agree that the game was invented to entertain the ruling class and to help them think about how to strategize in battle.

The Object of the Game

Two players compete in chess; one uses 16 light pieces, the other 16 dark pieces.

No matter what their actual color, the player with the light pieces is always called "White," while the one with the dark pieces is always "Black."

The object of the game is for one player to trap the other player's King.

How, you ask? That's what this chapter is all about.

Know the Territory

The chessboard is the battlefield where it all takes place. Think of it as your territory, the home that you need to defend!

It's a big square made up of 64 smaller squares – 32 light, 32 dark.

There are eight rows lined side-by-side, horizontally. These are called *ranks*.

And there are eight rows stacked up-and-down, vertically. These are called *files*.

Figure 2-1: A rank

Figure 2-2: A file

When you set up the board, check and make sure that the lower right corner for both players is a white square.

Remember this with a simple rhyme:
White on the right.

If you have a chess board and chess pieces, get them out now and set up the board in front of you. Follow along with your hands and you'll learn twice as fast.

Your Army

The chess pieces are the army you command. They protect your territory and your King, so get to know them well.

Each of the chess pieces has its own personal style. Some move forward, some move side-to-side, some move diagonally, and some can do combinations of moves.

Each player gets:

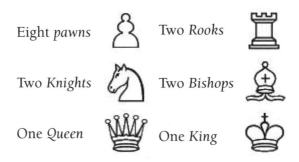

Eight *pawns*   Two *Rooks*

Two *Knights*   Two *Bishops*

One *Queen*   One *King*

The Right Words

When talking about chess, it's important to remember that there is a difference between "chess pieces" and "pieces."

The word "pieces" is used only to describe Rooks, Knights, Bishops and the Queen.

It can include the King as well, but he's usually just called "the King."

What matters here is that pawns are not pieces.

When I use the word "pieces" in this book, I'm *not* talking about pawns.

When I want to discuss the entire set, I'll use the words "chess pieces," which includes all the pieces and pawns.

This rule of thumb is often true whenever chess play is discussed, though sometimes "chessmen" is used instead of "chess pieces." I don't like the term "chessmen" though, because they're not all men!

You wouldn't want to upset the Queen would you?

So keep the words straight:

Pawns – The pawns.

Pieces – Rooks, Knights, Bishops, the Queen and (sometimes) the King.

Chess pieces – Any or all of the pieces and pawns.

A piece is a piece
A pawn is a pawn
The King is the King
And that's everything

One more note about naming: The Queen and Rooks are sometimes called the *major pieces*, while the Bishops and Knights are the *minor pieces*.

This is because, as you will see, the Queen and Rooks are more powerful than the Bishops and Knights.

Line Up!

The chess pieces are set up in two rows. The front row is made up of the eight pawns. To set up the back row:

1. Start by putting your two Rooks on the outside edges, one on the far left, one on the far right.

2. Next, moving from the outside in, fill in the six open squares between the Rooks. Put the two Knights beside the Rooks.

3. Put your Bishops beside the Knights.

4. Now only the two center squares are empty. This is where the King and Queen stand. But be careful, because their position changes depending on whether you're playing White or Black.

The key to remember is that the Queen is vain, and she likes her clothes to match her square.

So put her on the light square if she's the White Queen and on the dark square if she's the Black Queen. The King goes next to her.

Set your chess pieces into position now and check to make sure that they match this picture:

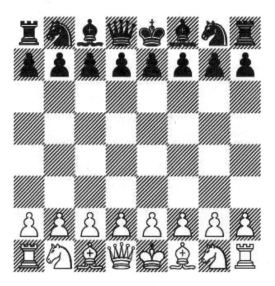

Figure 2-3: The chessboard set up for play. Notice that the bottom right square is a white square.

When you look at the board, imagine a vertical line running up and down, right through the middle, which splits the board in half between the Queens and the Kings.

The half with the Kings on it is called the *King's Side*, and the half with the Queens on it is called the *Queen's Side*.

The pieces on the King's half are named for him – the King's Bishop, King's Knight and King's Rook.

The pieces on the Queen's half are named for her – the Queen's Bishop, Queen's Knight and Queen's Rook.

Now, imagine a horizontal line running sideways through the middle of the board.

This is the Frontier Line.

It divides the territory into halves, one for White and one for Black.

Each player's half is four ranks–the two where the pieces and pawns stand at the beginning, and the two open ranks ahead of them.

Pass beyond the line and you're in enemy territory!

Figure 2-4: King's Side, Queen's Side, and the Frontier Line.

The Power of Each Piece

Now that your armies are ready, the battle begins!

All of the chess pieces are after the same thing: to weaken the defenses of the other side in order to trap the enemy King.

The chess pieces do this in two ways: By *controlling* squares and by *capturing* the other side's chess pieces.

Each chess piece captures another by moving into a square that an enemy chess piece occupies.

The captured piece or pawn is then taken off the board and removed from play.

Let's get to know each of your chess pieces individually and learn how each of them move, capture and control.

The King

The King is your main man. In most chess sets, he's the tall piece with the cross on his head.

The entire game is based around what happens to him.

With every move you make, you should be keeping two things in mind:

- Protect my King

- Go after my opponent's King

But the King has a problem. He's slow and he can't move around much. In fact, he can only move one square per turn.

But he can move in any direction: up, down, left, right, or diagonally. Like this:

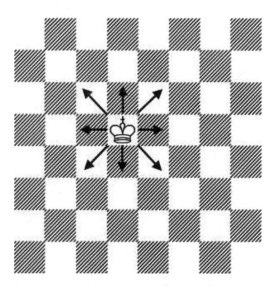

Figure 2-5: Movement of the King

The King can capture other pieces by moving into their square, but at the beginning of the game you shouldn't use him that way. He's not there to attack; leave that to his army.

Remember, half of the game is about defending your King.

So keep him safe and out of danger! He should be protected and hidden away, avoiding enemy chess pieces at all costs.

At the end of the game the King can come out to fight, but we'll get to that later.

The Queen

The King is the most important piece in the game, but his wife, the Queen, is the *strongest* piece. She towers over everyone else in ability. She's got the power, and she knows it!

The Queen can move up, down, left, right, diagonally–any direction she wants–along ranks, files and diagonals. She can also go as far as she wants in one move–one square, the entire length of the board and everything in between. She's the one piece your opponent fears most. Use her correctly and she will go a long way in helping you win the game.

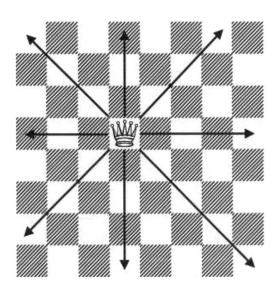

Figure 2-6: Movement of the Queen

The Rook

The two Rooks, sometimes called "castles" because they're shaped like the towers of a castle, start out on the outer edge of the board. Rooks move in straight horizontal or vertical lines, either along ranks or along files, like this:

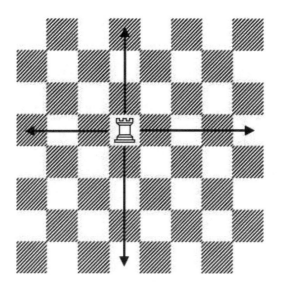

Figure 2-7: Movement of the Rook

Like the Queen, the Rook can move as many squares as he wants in one move. And while he can't move in diagonals, he's still the second most powerful piece in the game. He can dominate and control the entire rank or file he's on, no matter how far away he is from an enemy. He's powerful for both offense and defense, so use him wisely!

The Bishop

Bishops are the pieces shaped like a rounded pillar. They usually have a slit cut out of the top that looks like a frowning mouth (this is called a *mitre*). The Bishops are the "slanters" of the chess board because they only move in diagonals, never in straight lines along ranks or files. Like the Queen and Rook, they can move as far as they want in one move.

One of your Bishops starts on a light square, the other starts on a dark square, and neither one ever leave the color he starts on. This is important when you think about your Bishop and how to use him. Imagine one of them as the protector of the light squares, and the other as the protector of the dark squares.

Take a look and watch how he moves:

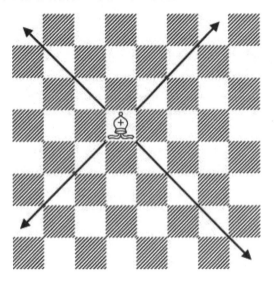

Figure 2-8: Movement of the Bishop

Because he can never leave his own color, he can't touch half of the board. The Bishop has less power than the Queen or the Rook, but that's not to say that he's weak. He can do a lot for you as long as you get him to work together with your other pieces.

The Knight

Your Knights are the pieces shaped like a horse's head. They're oddballs in a couple of ways. First, they don't move in straight lines or diagonals, but in an "L" shape. And, they always move exactly three squares: either two steps in one direction, then one step in another; or one step in one direction, then two steps in another.

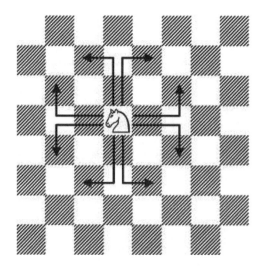

Figure 2-9: Movement of the Knight

The Knight can move wherever he wants, as long as it's in the shape of an "L." To be sure you're moving him correctly, remember this simple rule: If the Knight starts on a light square, he'll stop on a dark square; and, if he starts on a dark square, he'll stop on a light square. This is always true. If you've got your board in front of you, try it out. Move the Knight and say it out loud:

One, Two, Turn!
One, Two, Turn!
One, Two, Turn!
One, Two, Turn!

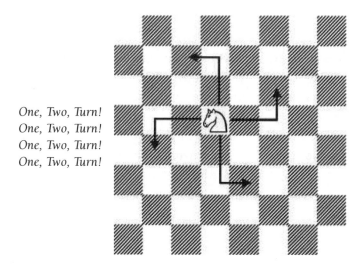

Figure 2-10

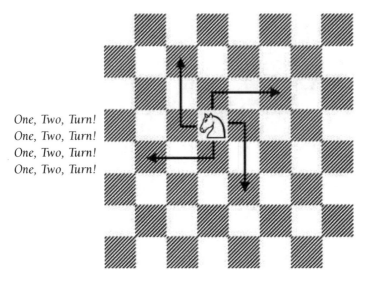

One, Two, Turn!
One, Two, Turn!
One, Two, Turn!
One, Two, Turn!

Figure 2-11

The second reason that the Knight is unusual is that he can jump over other pieces and pawns–your own *and* your opponent's. No other piece can do this. The Knight can only capture a piece in the square that he lands on, but unlike all other chess pieces, he can't get stuck. We'll discuss this more when we get to the rules of play.

The Pawn

Last but not least are the little ones that make up half of your army: the pawns. A pawn can move forward either one or two squares on his first move. On all moves after that, he can only move forward one square. Once you move a pawn forward, he can *never* go back, and he can't move sideways either. The only time a pawn moves in any way besides straight forward is when he's capturing. For captures he moves diagonally, taking the piece or pawn in the square to his upper left or upper right. A pawn can't capture or move around a chess piece that's directly in front of him.

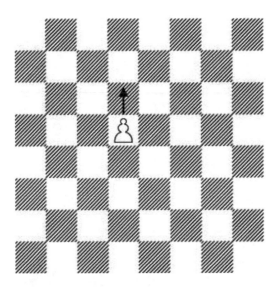

Figure 2-12: Movement of the pawn

Figure 2-13: Pawn capture

A Fancy Capture – Pawns can also take other pawns in a different way. It is called *en passant*. En passant is French for "in passing." Here's how it happens:

1. White's pawn has moved forward three squares, to the fifth rank.

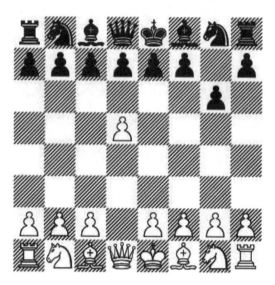

Figure 2-14

2. One of Black's pawns, on its first move, goes forward two squares and ends up on the fifth rank, on the file next to White's pawn.

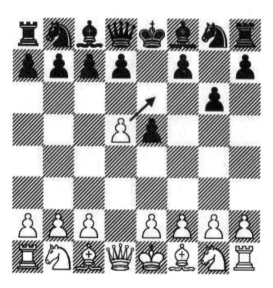

Figure 2-15: White can move into the square shown by the arrow, and take Black's pawn.

3. White moves forward diagonally and takes Black's pawn as if the pawn had only moved forward one square!

Figure 2-16

Other en passant rules:

1. Both Black and White can capture en passant.
2. Only pawns – not pieces – can capture or be captured en passant.
3. The pawn can only be captured after its first move, and it must be captured right away. This is a limited-time offer!

One thing you should remember is that many casual chess players don't even know about this move. It's a strange one. There is a good chance that at some point you will be playing against someone who has never heard of en passant. So don't be surprised if they accuse you of making what they think is an illegal move. If you have my book handy, show them this page and be sure to tell them that I'm a trained professional!

Up For Promotion – Pawns are weak most of the time, but down the road they can become very powerful. How? If the pawn can make it all the way to the last rank, he gets a promotion. You can now choose between 4 pieces to turn him into: a Rook, a Bishop, a Knight or a Queen (you can't turn him into a King, and he can't stay as a pawn). Once he's promoted, he stays promoted until the end of the game. Pawn promotion is also called Queening, because you'll almost always want to turn him into a Queen. After all, she is the most powerful piece. There are rare moments when you might want to promote to a Knight, and even rarer moments when you'll want to promote to a Rook or Bishop, but that's usually only done by advanced players. Stick to Queening for now.

Here's how to promote a pawn:

1. First, get your pawn to the last rank. (This is easier said than done!)

2. If your opponent has captured your Queen, take the pawn off the board and ask for your lady back. Now, put her where your pawn was.

3. If your opponent has *not* captured your Queen, have him give back one of your captured Rooks. Then turn the Rook upside down and place it on the board.

4. If your opponent hasn't captured your Queen or either of your Rooks, tip the pawn over and lay him down on his side.

5. If you want to promote your pawn into a Knight, Rook, or Bishop instead, replace him with one of your captured Knights, Rooks, or Bishops. If none have been captured, tip the pawn on his side.

A Complicated Man – A lot of beginning players don't like the pawn because of how little he can do and how strange he is when it comes to moving and capturing (especially en passant). Doesn't seem worth the trouble, does it?

Take it from an expert: You'll learn to appreciate your pawns. Sometimes just one pawn will make the difference between winning and losing.

Try not to look at what a pawn is; look at him for what he can be. A pawn has more potential than any other piece. He's got to go through a lot to get there, but if you manage to get a pawn Queened, there's a good chance that the game will turn in your favor.

Quick Review

King – Moves one square in any direction.

Queen – Moves any number of squares in straight lines along ranks and files, or along diagonals.

Rook – Moves any number of squares in straight lines along ranks and files.

Bishop – Moves any number of squares, only along diagonals.

Knight – Moves three squares in an "L" shape. One, two, turn!

Pawn – Moves one or two squares straight ahead on the first move, and only one square straight ahead on all following moves. Cannot move backward or side-to-side, and may only move diagonally when capturing. Can capture "en passant" if the conditions are right, and may be promoted to a Queen, Knight, Rook or Bishop if he makes it to the last rank.

Castling

There is one other chess move, called *castling*, which involves moving both the King and the Rook. This is the only move in chess where two chess pieces are moved at the same time. And it's extremely valuable to know!

Remember that the King is the most important person on the battlefield, and that he must be kept safe no matter what the cost. That's the idea behind castling. What you're doing is taking him out of the open and placing him closer to the side of the board, where it's harder for enemy pieces to get to him. Plus, it gets him behind the Rook, and under his guard. Here are the rules of castling:

1. Castling counts as one move and to do it, it must be your turn. Announce to your opponent that you are castling by saying "I castle" or "I'm castling."

2. Both the King and the Rook must stay in their starting squares until you castle. If you've moved either of them at all, castling is no longer allowed.

27

3. The two squares between the King and the Rook must be empty; in other words, the King's Knight and King's Bishop need to be moved out of their squares first.

4. The King must not be in the path of an enemy piece before or after he castles, and neither of the two open squares between the Rook and the King can be in the path of an enemy piece.

If you can make the move without breaking any of those rules, you're ready to castle. Here's how it's done:

1. Have the King walk two steps to the right toward his Rook. They should now be standing next to each other.

2. Take the Rook and have him jump to the left, over the King! The Rook lands in the square next to him.

Try it now. Remember, the King goes two steps to the right and the Rook jumps over him. Say it out loud:

One, Two, Jump!

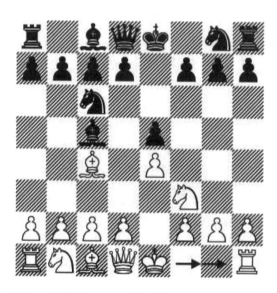

Figure 2-17: Start castling (One, Two...)

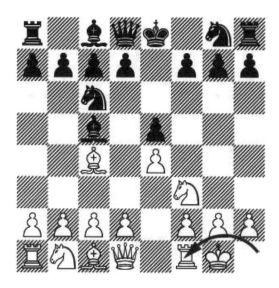

Figure 2-18: Finish! (Jump!)

This move is called *King's Side castling*, sometimes called "castling short." But you can also do a *Queen's Side castle* ("castling long"). The rules are the same, except that the Queen, the Queen's Bishop and the Queen's Knight must move out of their squares before you do it, leaving three open squares between the King and the Queen's Rook. Here's how to castle on the Queen's side:

1. The King takes two steps – but this time it's to the left, toward the Queen's Rook.

2. The Rook jumps one square further in a Queen's side castle. He leaps to the right over an open square, then over the King, and lands in the next square.

One, Two, Jump!

Figure 2-19: Start castling (One, Two...)

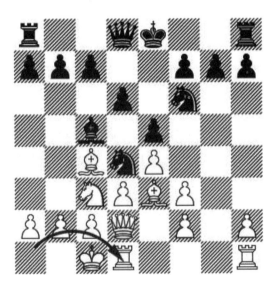

Figure 2-20: Finish! (Jump!)

As you can see, castling isn't hard to learn. You can play a game without ever doing it, and many people don't even know how to castle at all. But knowing this move puts you a step ahead of many casual players. That's because castling is one of the key moves in winning chess. You'll understand why later on.

Rules of the Road

Knowing how each of the chess pieces move is the foundation of chess. If you've gotten this far, you're almost ready to play. But there are a few more rules to go over.

White Goes First – The player with the white chess pieces always makes the first move of the game. Then Black moves, then White and so on until the end. There is no official rule stating how to choose which person will play White and which will play Black. You and your opponent may decide however you want.

Touch Move, Touch Take – If a player touches any of his chess pieces on his turn, then he *must* move the piece or pawn that he touched. If he touches more than one chess piece, then he must move the piece that he touched first. This isn't a good situation to be in! A beginner needs to learn patience and restraint. So don't touch any of your chess pieces until you're ready to move.

The Law is the Law – If you make an illegal move and the other player says so, you must retract the move and make a legal one with the same piece or pawn. If the illegal move was a capture, then the same capture must be made with another chess piece, if possible. Study and follow the rules of movement and this won't be a problem for you. But be on the lookout for other players making illegal moves, especially beginners. You don't want them to steal a move from you, whether or not they did it on purpose. If they steal one move, they may end up stealing the whole game!

No Sharing – No two chess pieces may be on the same square at the same time. If you move into a square that is occupied by an enemy piece or pawn, capture it and take its place. But you can't move into a square that one of your own chess pieces is already standing in.

Traffic Jam – No chess piece except the Knight can jump over or go around any other chess piece. When a piece or pawn can't move any further in a certain direction, it's called a *blockade*. At the beginning of the game, all the pieces in the back row are blockaded by the pawns lined up in front of them – except for the Knight (remember, he can jump over anybody).

Time Limit – In most personal games, there's no limit to the time a player can take to make his move, or how long a game can last. Some players are going to make you hate this rule! Certain opponents can stare at the board for 10 or 15 minutes before moving. On the other hand, having time to think can work in your favor.

This is not true of tournaments, however. In a tournament or public game, a chess clock is used. Each player gets a certain amount of time to make all of their moves, which differs depending on the game and the tournament. Some games give each player 40 moves over 2 hours. Other games, known as "blitz chess" give each player only 5 minutes! The clock starts running when each turn begins, and is paused when the player finishes his or her move. When the other player moves, the first player's clock starts running again. If one player's clock runs out, he or she is out of time and automatically loses the game.

Even though a time clock isn't required, I recommend that you buy one and play your games with it. The clock puts pressure on you to move, so it forces you to learn to think faster. And that's a skill everybody should develop.

How Does It All End?

A game of chess can end in one of many different ways. But the best way, and your goal, is to win with a checkmate. Let's look at how this happens.

Check!

If a player's King is in the path of one or more of the other player's chess pieces and can be captured on the attacking player's next move, then the King is in *check*. Usually the player announces this by saying "Check!" This is a warning. It means "I can capture your King, so get him out of danger right now." If you are in check, don't even think about anything but getting your King to safety! You've got three options:

1. *Escape* to a safe square;

2. *Block* the path of the attacking piece with another one of your pieces or pawns; or

3. *Capture* the piece that's threatening the King.

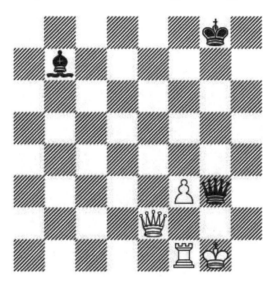

Figure 2-21: It is White's turn to move, and his King is in check. He is in the path of Black's Queen. White can't capture the Queen, but there are two things he can do to get out of check. Either:

1. Move his King one square to the right (escape)

2. Move his Queen two squares to the right, in front of Black's Queen (block)

Checkmate!

A checkmate is a check that can't be escaped with any one move. The piece or pieces attacking the King can't be avoided, blocked or captured. The King is stuck.

When this happens, the player who trapped the King says "Checkmate!" and wins the game.

Figure 2-22: Checkmate! There is nothing White can do. He is in the path of Black's Queen. He can't capture the Queen, escape to a safe square, or be blocked by any piece or pawn.

There are two important rules about being in check:

Move It Or Lose It – If a player's King is in check, that player *must* get out of check on his or her next move. If the player doesn't, then he or she automatically forfeits the game and loses.

Jumping Into the Fire – No player can make a move that puts his or her own King into check or checkmate. This is an illegal move, and it counts as an automatic loss. Here's an example.

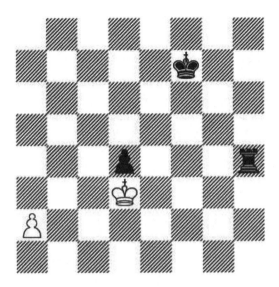

Figure 2-23: White's King wants to capture Black's pawn, but he can't. It would be illegal because he'd be stepping into check by Black's Rook.

Other Endings

Chess games don't always end with a checkmate. Here are the other ways in which a game can end:

Resignation – A player resigns when he or she has no hope of winning. The other player wins. If your position is bad, you've lost too many chess pieces or you see that there's a checkmate coming that's impossible to stop, you can end the game without fighting on to the end. A player resigns by tipping over his King and saying "I resign." However, I'm only telling you this because it's an official rule. For now, I don't ever want you to resign, especially if you're playing against someone new to chess! He or she might make enough mistakes so that you can still turn the game around and end up the winner.

Stalemate – A stalemate happens when *the King is the only chess piece a player can move, and the only possible move will put the King into check.* Remember, a King can't move into check! So, since the player can't make a legal move, the game ends here. Neither player wins or loses–the game just stops. Understanding stalemates, and avoiding them, is important. We'll go over some examples of stalemates in Chapter 9.

Drawn Games – A draw is different than a stalemate, but the result is the same. There is no winner, no loser. Here are the four ways in which a game ends in a draw (tie):

1. **Threefold repetition** – The game ends in a draw if the exact same board position is repeated three times.

2. **The Fifty Moves Rule** – If fifty moves have gone by since the last capture, or since the last time a pawn moved, the game is a draw.

3. **Perpetual Check** – If one side can keep checking the other player's King, forcing him to move back and forth, the game is a draw that will end because of threefold repetition. This is called perpetual check. Often a player will try to force a draw by perpetual check when he or she is in trouble, or knows that winning is impossible.

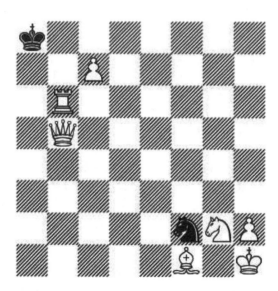

Figure 2-24: All White has to do is move his Queen one square to the left to get a checkmate and win. But White's King is checked by Black's Knight! The rules say he must get his King out of check, even if he could checkmate Black on the next move.

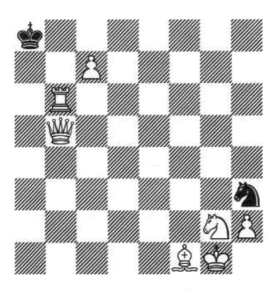

Figure 2-25: White gets out of check by moving his King one square to the left. But Black responds by moving her Knight (one, two, turn) to check again!

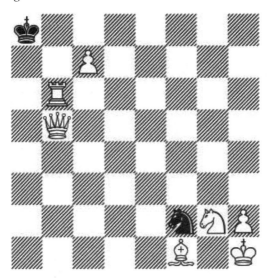

Figure 2-26: Look familiar? White moves his King one square to the right to escape check, and Black's Knight leaps right back to check him again! Once this position repeats three times, the game will end in a draw. This is some crafty playing by Black. She saw that she was only one move away from being checkmated, so she forced a perpetual check!

4. **Agreed Draw** – Last but not least is the agreed draw. If both players agree, for whatever reason, to stop playing, the game is a draw.

There are many reasons to agree to a draw. There may not be enough pieces left to force a checkmate. Maybe it's just a boring game. Whatever the reason, the game stops without a winner.

Ready to Roll

Congratulations! Now you know the rules of chess. Don't worry about remembering all of them. And expect to make some mistakes at first. It's a lot to keep straight. The important thing is to remember just enough so that you can play, and to keep this book nearby if you forget something or become confused. Eventually, when you've played enough games, it will all become habit.

You've learned everything you need in order to play casual games against your friends and family. But you're not going to play very well unless you keep reading! So don't close the book yet, especially if you're confused. If you want to play like a pro, there's a whole lot more to learn.

Chapter 3

Put it on Paper

Many people say that Bobby Fischer is the greatest chess player of the last century. If you want to see how he plays, you don't need a video, pictures or even diagrams of any kind.

Just open any of the books that discuss his games and you'll see his every move right there in front of you.

That's because somebody wrote them down.

A game of chess isn't like a game of football or basketball, where fans only remember the final score and maybe a few good plays.

With chess, every single move can be recorded on paper, read and played again later with a simple notation system.

Records of the Battle

So how do you "write" or "read" a game of chess?

Don't worry. It's easier than learning the alphabet or memorizing multiplication tables; in fact, it's no harder than simply learning how the pieces move.

Think of this: If you want to build a house, you first imagine it in your mind. Then you put it on paper, as a blueprint, and work from that.

After all, if you build a home based only from a mental image, you might forget something important – like the bathroom! Paper doesn't forget.

So take the thoughts, memories and events out of your brain and write them down.

In the case of chess, this means recording your games so that they will be the blueprint for your future learning and improvement.

Why Chess Notation is Important

A Common Language – Whenever a chess game is discussed in writing – whether in books, newspapers or on the Internet – chess notation is used as a simple, universal way of telling the reader which moves the chess pieces are making.

This is very important, as the author must be able to communicate in a way that's quick, easy to read and exact.

The rest of this book is full of chess strategies and tips, written in chess notation. So if you want to understand my words, you're going to have to learn the language!

Learn from Your Own Play – Analyzing your past games is the key to finding your strengths and weaknesses.

Take a look at my experience: I played in the Chess World Open in Philadelphia, Pennsylvania and won 6 of 9 games. When it was all over I went home and studied my games (games are recorded in all chess tournaments) and, because everything had been recorded, I could easily see exactly what I did wrong – or even right!

I attained knowledge and wisdom from not only my failures, but from my successes as well.

Learn from Other Players – Studying your opponent's moves can teach you a lot; studying the games of the great chess masters can teach you even more.

Thanks to chess records, it's easy to take a look at an "instant replay" of games that took place yesterday, last month or even hundreds of years ago. If you study what the masters do, you can share in their wisdom and experience.

Following the examples of others can help you grow as a player, and might even help you avoid unnecessary mistakes. That's the magic of having everything on paper.

Charting the Territory

Every one of the 64 squares on a chess board has its own name.

Each file (remember, files are the up-and-down columns) is named from left to right with a letter from **a** to **h**. Each rank (side-to-side row) is named, bottom to top, with a number from **1** to **8**.

Getting the name of each square is simple. You take the letter of the file, and then add the number of the rank.

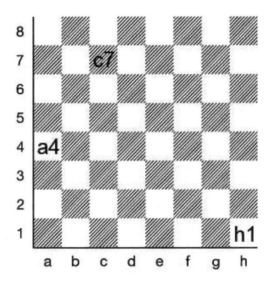

Figure 3-1: Squares a4, c7 and h1. For practice, try finding and pointing out squares b3, d6 and h5.

If you can find and name the squares, you're halfway to understanding the language of chess notation.

I told you it was easy!

Recording the Action

In chess notation, each piece is named by a letter. To write down the movement of the pieces, you first write the piece's letter, and then the square that it moved to.

This is how it works:

Letter	Example
K - King	**Ke3** (King has moved to square **e3**)
Q - Queen	**Qh2** (Queen has moved to square **h2**)
R - Rook	**Rg4** (Rook has moved to square **g4**)
B - Bishop	**Ba6** (Bishop has moved to square **a6**)
N - Knight	**Nf3** (Knight has moved to square **f3**)
Pawn	**e4** (pawn has moved to square **e4**)

Did you notice that there's no letter for the pawn? That's because a pawn isn't notated with one.

All that's written down is the square that he moves to.

You might have also noticed that we use an **N** for the Knight (sometimes you might see **Kn** used). That's because **K** is already being used for the King.

In a written chess game, there are two columns. White's moves are recorded in the left column, and Black's moves are recorded in the right column.

Wait a Minute . . . Which Rook Moved?!

Let's say that you read **Nc3** in White's column on a list of moves. Then **e4**. You think to yourself "There are two Knights and eight pawns. How do I know which ones are moving?"

Simple.

The Knight can only move three squares at a time, and **c3** is on the Queen's side of the board. So, there's no way that the King's Knight could have legally made this move!

We know it was the Queen's Knight, because only he could have moved there. The same goes for e4; since pawns can only move forward, only the pawn on the e file could have made that move.

The point is that the notation doesn't tell you everything. But it tells you enough so that if you know the rules of movement, there will almost never be a question about which piece or pawn is moving where.

Well, *almost* never.

Every now and then there will be times when there are two pieces that could have made the same move.

Let's say you're playing White and both of your Rooks are placed in rank 1, with no chess pieces between them, like this:

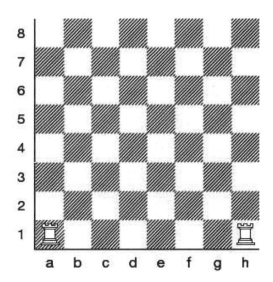

Figure 3-2: Both Rooks are in rank 1.

Then you move one of your Rooks from square h1 to square f1 . . .

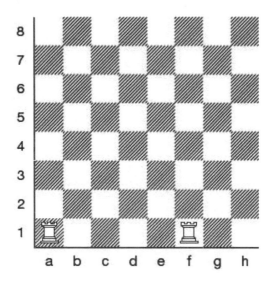

Figure 3-3: Moving a Rook from square h1 to f1.

. . . and then write **Rf1** in the notation. But wait – since both Rooks can travel in straight lines across ranks or files, that move could have been made by either of your two Rooks!

Since **f1** is a square either of your rooks could legally move to, a person reading your game wouldn't know whether you moved your **a1** Rook or your **h1** Rook.

At times like this, you have to be sure the move is clear, so the correct notation is to *put the Rook's starting square in parentheses.*

For example, instead of simply noting **Rf1**, you would want to write **R(h)f1**. That tells the reader that "the Rook starting on **h1** moved to **f1**."

Game Symbols

Aside from piece and pawn movement, there are a few other symbols used in chess notation.

They are:

Symbol	Meaning	Example
x	Capture	**Qxh4**. This means that the Queen has made a capture on square **h4**. Most of the time, the piece or pawn that was taken isn't notated, only that there was a capture. (In some recorded games, you will see the name of the piece noted as well.) When a pawn makes a capture, the pawn is named by the file that it started on. The notation **axb4** would mean that "the pawn on file **a** moved and captured the piece or pawn on **b4**."
0-0	King's side castle	**0-0**. No other numbers or letters are used.
0-0-0	Queen's side castle	**0-0-0**.
+	The King is in check	**Rf7+**. This means that the Rook has moved to square **f7** and has checked the enemy King.
#	Checkmate	**Qh3#**. Lights out! Checkmate. The game is over. Sometimes the symbol **++** is used.
e.p.	En passant capture	**dxe5e.p.** The pawn on file **d** captured the pawn on **e5** en passant.

Good Move! (Or Not?)

This next group of symbols isn't as important to remember if you're recording a game yourself, but you will see them in many professional notations:

! - A smart move

!! - A brilliant move

? - A bad move

?? - A *really* bad move

?! - A move made when a better move was possible

Let's say that the Rook who checked the other player's King on **f7** took a Bishop when he got there. Then we would write: **Rxf7+**.

Now, let's say that, by doing this, the player left his own King open for a quick check or checkmate! Then we would write **Rxf7+??**, as it was a *really* bad move to allow his King to be so vulnerable.

Always Play Along

When you're reading a recorded game, it's a good idea to follow the written moves with your own chess board and chess pieces.

Otherwise, you'll have to picture the board and the moves in your mind. And unless you have an incredible memory, it will be very difficult to keep up.

Let's Read a Game

If any of this seems confusing so far, don't worry. You're going to read an example game now, and when you do you'll see just how easy it is.

The following are the notations from a game I played with Russian International Master Rashid Ziyatdinov.

Don't worry about the reasons behind each move now; later on we'll come back and analyze it one move at a time.

For now, just remember to follow along with your own board and check the diagrams as you go. If your board doesn't match the picture, look again carefully and try to figure out when and how you made the mistake.

1.   e4   e5

Again, pawns have no letter in chess notation. You only write the square that they move to.

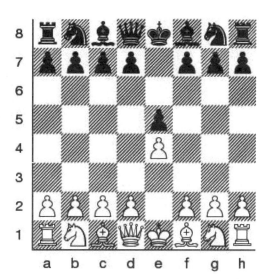

Figure 3-4

2.   Nf3   Nc6

Remember, the letter for the Knight is N, not K!

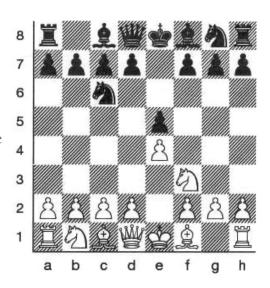

Figure 3-5

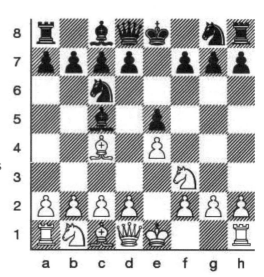

3.　　　Bc4　　Bc5

Knowing which Bishop
moved is never a problem,
because one stays on the
light squares; the other stays
on the dark squares.

Figure 3-6

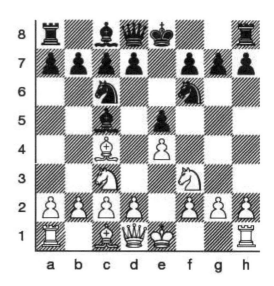

4.　　　Nc3　　Nf6

My King's Knight can't
possibly move to **Nc3**;
the same goes for Rashid's
Queen's Knight moving
to **Nf6**.

Do you see why?

Figure 3-7

5.   d3   d6

A pawn can only move forward, except when capturing. As long as you know this, you'll never make a mistake about which pawn is moving when recording or reading a game.

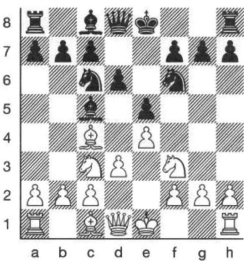

Figure 3-8

6.   Be3   Bg4

Now my light square Bishop and Rashid's dark square Bishop move out.

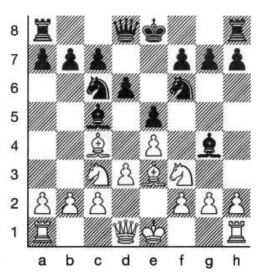

Figure 3-9

7.   Qd2   Bxf3

Rashid has made a capture!
Which piece was it?

The notation doesn't say,
but if you've followed
along, you'll know.

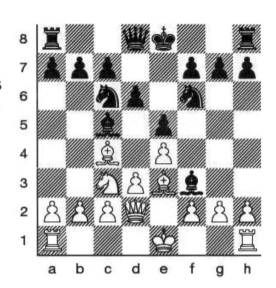

Figure 3-10

8.   gxf3   Nd4

Remember that a lower-case
letter before the x means
that it's a pawn making the
capture. The letter shows
the file that the pawn moved
from.

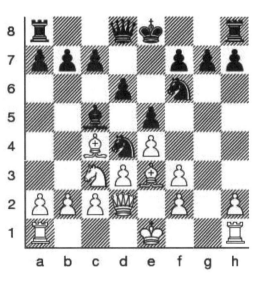

Figure 3-11

9.   Bxd4   Bxd4

Both of us made exactly the same move! It can happen.

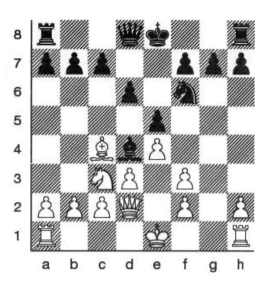

Figure 3-12

10.   0-0-0   c6

I made a Queen's Side castle. Notice that there are no letters or numbers; there's no need.

Castling always involves the same two pieces (Rook and King) and the squares they move to are the same every time.

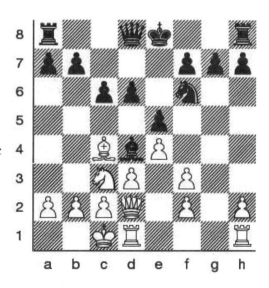

Figure 3-13

11.   R(h)g1   b5

Do you see why the **h** is in parentheses?

Because either one of my Rooks could have moved to **g1**. The letter **h** tells you which of the two it was.

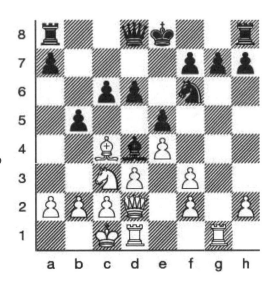

Figure 3-14

12.   Bb3   a5

Hopefully it's coming easier to you by now.

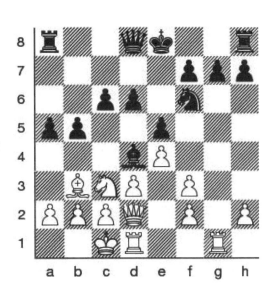

Figure 3-15

13.   a3   b4

More pawn movement.

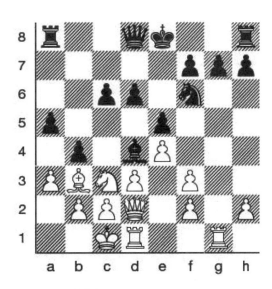

Figure 3-16

14.   axb4   axb4

Once again we make the same move, one right after the other!

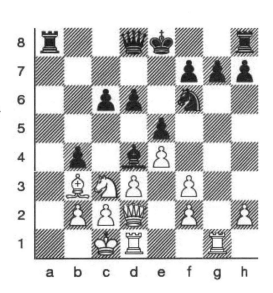

Figure 3-17

15.   Nb1   0-0

This time it's Rashid who castles, and he does it on King's side.

Be sure that you know the difference between 0-0 (King's side castle) and 0-0-0 (Queen's side castle).

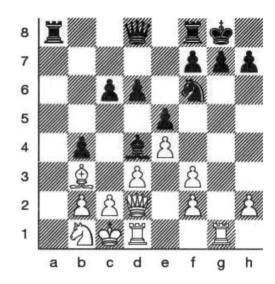

Figure 3-18

16.   Qh6   Ne8??

Rashid made a losing move here, which is why he gets the two question marks.

But how do you know when to add question marks when you're recording a game?

It's not so important for you to be able to do it at this stage of your learning, as long as you know what it means when you see it.

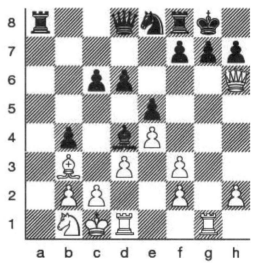

Figure 3-19

17.   Rxg7!!   Nxg7

Now a brilliant move from me – and it's not just my opinion. When I recorded this game into a computer, it added this symbol automatically!

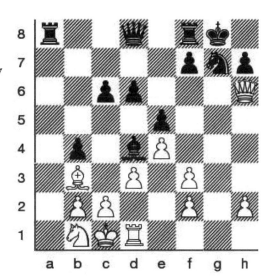

Figure 3-20

18.   Rg1   resigns

This is the end of our game.

Congratulations! You're ready to read and record chess games.

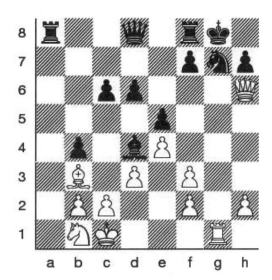

Figure 3-21

Other Notations

There's actually more than one system for chess notation.

The one I taught you in this chapter is called *Algebraic notation*. Algebraic is the one that's most commonly used today all over the world, and the one we will be using throughout the rest of this book.

But sometimes you may come across another, older way of writing games called the *English System*. I want to keep things simple, so I won't teach it to you in this book, but keep this in mind: the English system is like the tape cassette of the chess world; Algebraic notation is like the compact disc!

Why use old technology if there's something newer and better?

Lastly, there's a system known as *Full Algebraic*, in which the starting square and ending square of each move are noted, but no symbol is given for the pieces.

For example, the first four moves of the game I showed you above would be written as:

1. e2-e4   e7-e5
2. g1-f3   b8-c6

Computer games sometimes use this system. But in some ways it's harder to follow, and it's very hard to keep the pieces straight in your mind if you aren't watching the game.

For now, let's just stick to the Algebraic system. There are many other books and web sites that can teach you more about the other systems if you want to learn them.

Chapter 4

Target Practice

N ow you understand the rules of the game of chess.

You also know how chess pieces move, and how to read common chess notation.

Be proud!

Because even if you haven't played a game yet, you've already taken your learning farther than many chess players ever go.

Hopefully you're having fun so far, because it's about to get even better.

Using Your Imagination

Now that you've gotten the hang of how the game works, you need some practice. There's no better way to get the movements and chess notation straight in your mind than to get some hands-on experience.

That's the first goal of this chapter.

But you also need to start learning to visualize.

Visualization means to see something in your mind that isn't actually there in front of you.

When you visualize, you try to see possibilities and future outcomes. You imagine, and you create mental pictures.

In chess, visualizing is extremely important; in fact, it is the real art of the game. The better you are at visualizing, the better you will be at chess.

The ability to visualize isn't something you're born with. Everybody has some degree of natural ability, but it's mostly something you develop with practice.

So this chapter is also about starting you down the road of visualization.

How are we going to do that?

By going on a pawn hunt!

Test Drive Your Army

This is a series of six simple mini games to help you learn about each of the chess pieces.

After all, the chess pieces are your friends and allies! You should get to know them as well as you can before taking them into battle.

Each chess piece has its own spirit and personality. Try these games and you'll begin to discover them.

The games are simple to play, and go a long way in building your chess confidence.

Playing the Pawn Hunt Games

You will need:

1. A board and chess pieces. If you don't have them, use the pictures in the book and trace your movements with your finger.

2. A piece of paper and a pen. With these you will record each of your moves.

The key to each of these games is to think before you make a move.

Just like in a real game of chess, you need to have a plan for where you're going and what you're doing before you actually touch the piece to move it.

This is where visualization comes in!

Make your moves only after you've been able to visualize them clearly in your mind.

Pawn Hunting: Rook

Set up the board so that it looks like this picture:

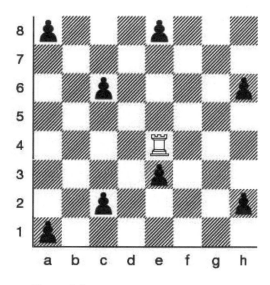

Figure 4-1

Your goal is to capture all of the pawns in no more than ten moves.

There is more than one correct way to do this!

As you capture each pawn, write down the move on your paper.

For example, if your first move is **Rxe3**, write it down. If your second move is **Re1** write that on the next line.

Keep these questions in mind as you hunt with the Rook:

- Can you plan out everything you're going to do before actually making a move?

- What might happen if you *don't* plan your moves in advance?

- How many different ways can you think of to capture the pawns?

Here is one possible solution to the game:

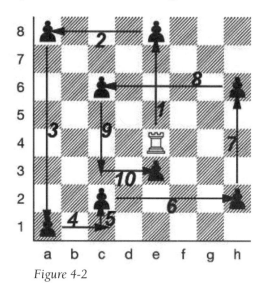

Figure 4-2

I captured the pawns in ten moves, but it's also possible to capture all the pawns in nine moves. Can you figure out how?

Pawn Hunting: Bishop

Here's how to set up the board:

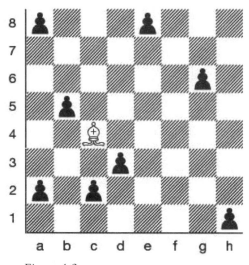

Figure 4-3

The goal here is to capture all eight pawns in no more than eleven moves.

As before, write down every move.

Here are some questions to think about for this game:

- Do you see the kinds of things the Bishop can do that the Rook can't?

- Do you see how and why the Bishop is a weaker piece than the Rook?

- Put a pawn on a dark square and try capturing it. Do you see the problem?

As you play, notice that even though the Bishop is capturing just as many pawns as the Rook, he doesn't get around as easily!

Here is one possible solution to the game:

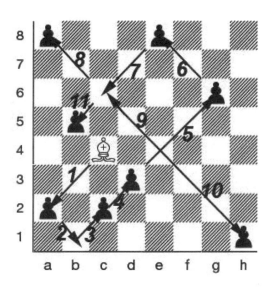

Figure 4-4

Can you capture all of the pawns in only ten moves?

It's possible. See if you can find a way!

Pawn Hunting: Knight

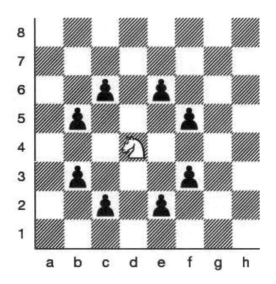

Figure 4-5

The Bishop game may have seemed a bit tricky, but this one's easy.

Your job is to capture the pawns one at a time, hopping back to your starting square after each capture.

But there's a twist. There are two ways to get your Knight back home: The way you came, and one other.

Get your Knight back by taking the second route.

Don't worry about counting the number of moves you take in this game, but do record your moves.

You can capture the pawns in any order you want. Remember, it's always **one, two, turn!**

Take a look at how the Knight can move in a circle. It's true that his steps go in an "L" shape, but he actually has the potential to make bolder movements than anyone else.

No other chess piece influences the board quite the same way as the Knight – not even the Queen!

This exercise is a good way to really study the Knight and to think about the sorts of things he can do for you.

Next, look at the two diagrams below:

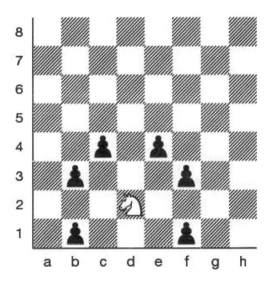

Figure 4-6

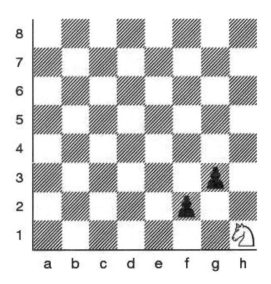

Figure 4-7

Notice anything?

The Knight can only take six pawns in Figure 4-6, and only two in Figure 4-7!

What does this mean?

The closer the Knight is to the sidelines, the less potential he has for movements and captures. But the closer he is to the center of the board, the more potential he has to move in a complete circle.

That's why some say *a Knight on the rim is dim!*

Later we're going to be talking about the importance of the center of the board in chess games.

You're already beginning to understand one reason for it, as you can see here why the center is the best place for the Knight to be.

Pawn Hunting: King

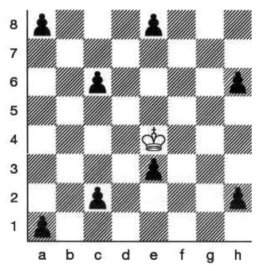

Figure 4-8

This one is going to try your patience!

The pawns are in the same place as they were in the Rook game, but it's going to take you many, many moves to finish, since the King can only move one square at a time.

He's like a snail, slowly sliding toward the pawns.

It's a good thing they can't run away!

For this game, only record your captures. Writing down every move would take too much time.

Be sure to count how many moves it takes you to finish. Then, compare that number to the games you played with the other pieces.

Big difference, isn't it?

- Do you see why the King is such a weak attacker?
- Do you see how difficult it is for the King to move away from threats and why he needs to be protected?

Pawn Hunting: Queen

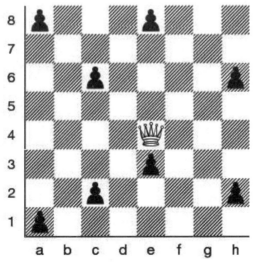

Figure 4-9

The goal in this game is to capture all of the pawns, in any way you want.

Count and record your moves.

When you finish, reset the board and do it again, but take a different route the second time.

As you move her around, notice how free you feel. You can do almost anything!

Starting to understand the power of the Queen?

- Do you see why you need to keep your Queen from being captured for as long as possible?
- Do you see why getting your pawns to the last rank where they can be promoted to the Queen's power ("Queened") is worth all the trouble?

This game can be finished in as little as eight moves, with a capture in each move!

See if you can find the solution.

Pawns Against Pawns

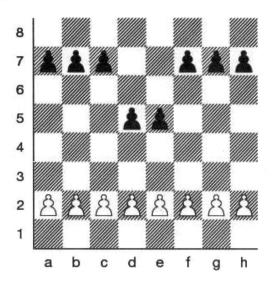

Figure 4-10

This game is a little trickier.

You play the White pawns and are going up against a line of Black's target dummy pawns.

Don't be afraid; they won't fight back!

You have three goals in this game:

1. Capture the six pawns on **a7**, **b7**, **c7**, **f7**, **g7** and **h7**.

2. Capture the two pawns on **d5** and **e5** en passant.

3. All of your pawns must end the game lined up next to each other on rank 7, like this:

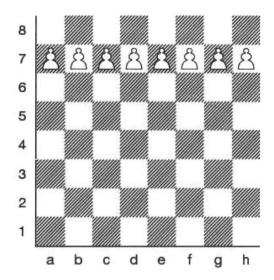

Figure 4-11

Here are some tips:

- You can make your moves in any order you want, as long as they're the correct ones. The result will be the same.

- If you try to capture Black's **c** and **f** pawns with your **b** and **g** pawns, you won't be able to line up on the seventh rank! Can you see the mistake?

- Remember, pawns can move forward *two* squares on their first move. Be sure to do it with each of your pawns.

- Remember that pawns capture diagonally.

- Take a look back at Chapter 2 if you've forgotten how to capture en passant.

Record all of your moves, but don't worry about how many you're making.

This game takes 32 moves to complete; each of the eight pawns will move exactly 4 times.

There are a few correct ways to complete this game. Try and find them.

Good luck!

Chapter 5

The Art of War

Knowing how each of the chess pieces gets around and seeing what they're capable of is only the first step of mastering chess.

The next is to understand the purpose behind it all.

Chess is like a dance; one piece moves a certain way, and the opponent's piece responds to that movement.

This chapter is about how the chess pieces dance with one another.

What are they trying to do, and why, with each move that they make?

The Metal of Your Armor

Your chess pieces, together, are like a suit of armor. The pieces and pawns are the metal, or *material*, that makes up your suit.

At the beginning of the game, your armor is sturdy and shiny. But as you play and lose material, your armor gets dents and holes punched into it.

Position, or *board position*, is a word that you'll often hear chess players use. It means: "where all the chess pieces are standing at any point in the game."

The diagrams in this book show the positions of chess pieces.

For example, Figure 2-3 shows the opening position, and Figure 2-22 shows a checkmate position.

Also, a player who is doing poorly might say that he has "poor position," and the other player could say that she has a "winning position."

Sometimes it'll be a bad position for both players, like when there are a lot of cramped chess pieces on both sides.

But the position changes with every move, and you should always look carefully at a game's position as a whole, not just where *your* chess pieces are.

As you will learn, making a good position for yourself is the key to winning!

Now that you've played with your chess pieces a little, you should be getting a sense of the value and importance of each piece, and how different they are from each other.

Because of this, some players rate their material by points:

A Pawn is worth 1 point
A Knight is worth 3 points
A Bishop is worth 3 points
A Rook is worth 5 points
The Queen is worth 9 points

The King isn't included on this list because his value can't be measured. If he's captured, the game ends.

In a way, losing your King is like losing your head. If that happened, you'd die no matter what shape your armor was in!

Combined, your chess army is worth 39 points of material.

As you can see by doing some simple math, the Queen is worth almost two Rooks; she's worth the same as three Bishops or Knights; and she's worth slightly more than one Rook and any other 3-point piece combined.

She's worth more than all of your pawns put together!

These point values may be useful to you as you play, but it's important to remember two things.

1. If any one soldier in your army can pull off something great, right then and there, that makes him more valuable than anyone else for that moment. Even a pawn can be your most valuable player, if the conditions are right.

   So while each chess piece has its own worth, overall they each will have their own time to shine.

2. A chess game is *not* scored. A checkmate is the goal, and it doesn't matter how many points your army is worth at the end.

   Points are just a way to help you think about the value of your chess pieces.

Win, Lose or Trade

Each player's material in a chess game is lost in two ways - captures or *exchanges*.

Your opponent loses material when you capture his or her pieces and pawns; and you lose material when he or she captures yours.

The two of you putting dents into each other's armor by knocking out material is a big part of the game!

And another big part of the game is exchanges, which can be *equal* or *inequal*.

Equal Exchanges

An equal exchange is a series of two to three moves where both players lose material, but each one gives up the same amount as the other.

Usually this means that two pieces of the same rank are lost.

Here's an example of an equal exchange:

Figure 5-1: *The two Queens stare each other down*

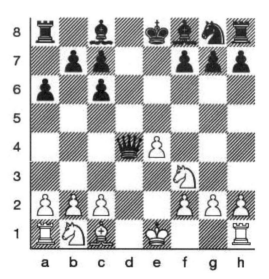

Figure 5-2: *Qxd4 - Black takes White's Queen!*

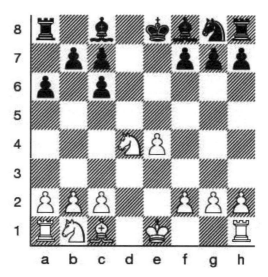

Figure 5-3: Nxd4 - White's Knight then replies by taking Black's Queen.

In this example, the two players have lost the same amount of material - their Queens.

It's bad news for both Black and White, but at least it's even. Neither of the players are left with any advantage over the other after this exchange.

Equal exchanges are often an accident, meaning that one player doesn't see the reply coming.

But there are moments in chess when it almost becomes a cooperative game, when the two players make equal exchanges with each other on purpose.

It may be that there are just too many pawns on the board blocking other pieces, so you decide to take an opponent's pawn, even though you know he's going to take yours right back. You both lose material, but it works out for the best because it clears out the board a little.

Even in competition there are times to work together for the good of both players.

Inequal Exchanges

An inequal exchange usually happens when one player makes a mistake.

He or she isn't paying attention to the board and makes a weak capture. Then, the other player swoops in and takes a more valuable piece.

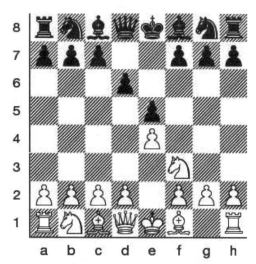

Figure 5-4: White's Knight (f6) has his eye on Black's pawn (e5).

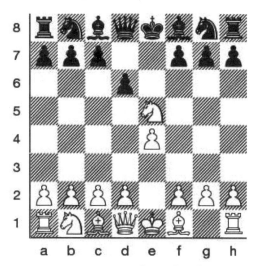

Figure 5-5: Nxe5 - White takes the pawn. But he didn't look closely enough before making this move!

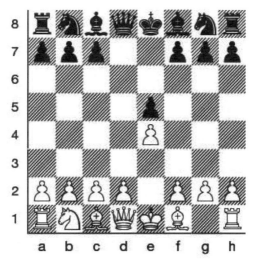

*Figure 5-6: **dxe5** - Black's pawn then takes White's Knight.*

White took a Black pawn, but lost a Knight. See? He lost 3 points for taking only 1 point, making it an inequal exchange.

This was a careless play by White, and now he's going to have some catching up to do!

Guarding

In Figure 5-4, you can see how Black's **d6** pawn is ready to take White's Knight on the next move – just in case White decides to attack **e5**.

This is called *guarding* or defending. It means that if a capture is made there can be instant retaliation.

Unfortunately, White went ahead and took the **e5** pawn anyway – and he lost his Knight to the **d6** pawn because of it.

Instant retaliation!

Keep your pieces guarded. It will make your opponent think twice before capturing them.

Threatening

A piece or pawn is *threatened* when it's in the path of one of the other player's chess pieces and can be captured on the next move.

If the threatened piece is not guarded, we say that the piece is *en prise* (pronounced *on preez*).

Like en passant, en prise is a French term. It means "in grip."

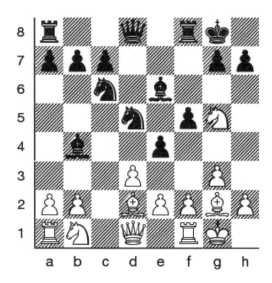

Figure 5-7: The battle is ready! In this diagram, Black and White's dark-square Bishops are threatening each other, and so are their pawns on d3 and e4. White's Knight (g5) is threatening one, two, three of Black's chess pieces! (The e4 pawn, e6 Bishop and h7 pawn.) Black's Queen is threatening the Knight.

Let's say you were playing Black in the above example and it were your turn to move.

What would you say is the smartest play?

- If you said **Qxg5**, think again.
  - Yes the Knight is threatening three of your chess pieces, but sending your Queen out to capture the Knight would be a huge mistake.
  - The **g5** square is guarded by White's dark-square Bishop. The Bishop would capture the Queen on the next move for a very inequal exchange of material.

- **Bxd2** is also not a good move.
  - The White Bishop is guarded by White's Knight and Queen. There's no doubt that one of them would take your Bishop right back.
  - Note that your Bishop is safe anyway; he's guarded by a Knight. Neither of these Bishops would be smart to attack the other; it would only result in a useless exchange.
- **exd3** isn't as bad a move as it might seem.
  - Yes, the pawn you'd take is guarded by another pawn, which would probably capture you right back – but there are two reasons why this would be okay:
    - First, it's an equal exchange – a pawn for a pawn.
    - Second, and most important, the recapture will weaken White's pawn structure and you'd be clearing a square on White's King's side. That means he'd be just a little more vulnerable to attack.
  - From there, maybe you could look a few moves deep and work out a plan.

The best move?

Do something about the Knight's threat to your Bishop on **e6**.

Bring your Rook or Queen out to protect the square, or keep it simple and just move the Bishop away.

There's no need to worry about the Knight capturing your **e4** or **h7** pawns.

Do you see why?

By now you probably do. If not, look again.

You'll improve at "reading" positions as you get more practice.

The important lesson for now is: *just because you can capture another piece does NOT mean that it's the best move, or even a good move.*

Even though Black has as many possible captures as he could make, the best possible move here is to not capture at all.

It seems obvious enough, but try to avoid making moves that put your chess pieces under threat, unless:

- The piece or pawn will be guarded;
- You want to make an equal exchange; or
- You want to sacrifice something for the sake of a plan.

Controlling

Any one of a player's chess pieces, when not totally blockaded, will always have at least one square that it can move to.

The squares that a chess piece can attack on its next move are squares that the chess piece *controls*.

Controlling can be very powerful, especially when it comes to the enemy King!

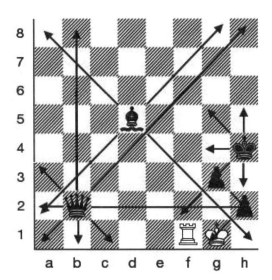

Figure 5-8: The arrows show the squares Black's chess pieces are controlling. White's King is checkmated here. The pawn on h2 gives check, while the Queen, Bishop and another pawn control all of White's escape squares.

Pinning

A piece is *pinned* when moving it would expose a more valuable piece to being captured.

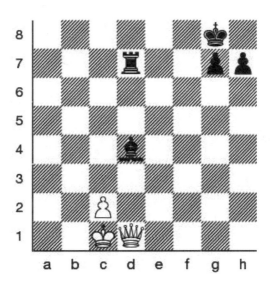

Figure 5-9: Black's Bishop better not move! If he does, his Rook will be captured by White's Queen.

The best thing about a pin for you, and the worst thing about it for your opponent, is that it makes the pinned piece useless! It's almost like a loss of material.

The Black Bishop in Figure 5-9 isn't free to do anything. If he moves, the White Queen will take the Rook.

An *absolute pin* is when moving a piece would expose the King to check.

Since that would be illegal, the player couldn't move the piece even if he wanted to.

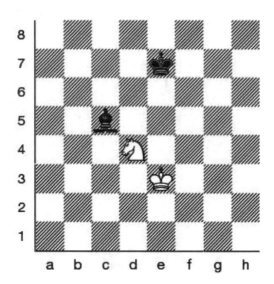

Figure 5-10: If the White Knight moves, the Black Bishop will be checking the King. The Knight's not going anywhere.

Fork

A *fork* is when a chess piece is threatening two or more enemy chess pieces at the same time.

Any chess piece can fork, even the pawn.

With Knights, forks are especially powerful. Since the Knight can hop over other chess pieces, many forks can happen even on crowded boards.

It's one of the Knight's favorite things to do.

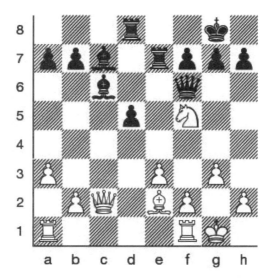

Figure 5-11: The White Knight is forking the Black Rook on e7 and the pawn on g7.

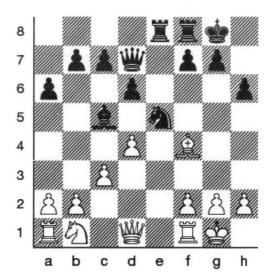

Figure 5-12: The White pawn on d4 forks the Black Bishop on c5 and Black Knight on e5.

When a Knight forks more than two pieces at once, it's called a *family fork*.

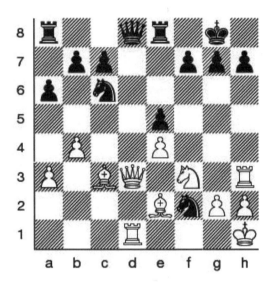

Figure 5-13: The Black Knight on f2 is forking both of White's Rooks, his Queen and is checking his King! Like it or not, White must get his King out of check by moving to g1.

A fork is one of the best positions for a chess player to be in.

It can take some work and smart planning to get yourself there, but once it happens, you don't want to be in your opponent's shoes!

Discovered Check

If you really want to cause some trouble in your opponent's position, try one of these two moves: a discovered check or a double check.

A *discovered check* is when one of your chess pieces stands between the enemy King and another of your pieces.

All you need to do is to move your middleman and . . . surprise! Check!

The best time to move that middle piece is when the move will threaten an enemy chess piece. Since the other player has no choice but to get their King out of check, the threatened piece or pawn is doomed.

Let's take a look at how this works:

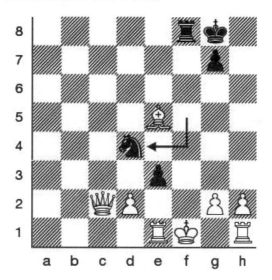

Figure 5-14: Nd4

Black has just hit White hard.

Moving the Knight opens up a path for the Rook and White's King is now in check.

Even worse, The Black Knight is now threatening the White Queen and there's nothing White can do about it!

The Bishop on **e5** can't capture the Knight because the King is in check and must be moved.

White is going to lose his Queen.

Double Check

A *double check* is just what it sounds like. It's when two chess pieces threaten the enemy King at the same time.

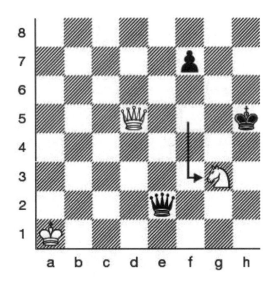

Figure 5-15: Ng3

Black's King is now in check from both the White Knight and the Queen.

The best part for White is that he's also threatening the Black Queen!

Again, Black has no choice but to get his King out of check.

Pawn Structure

When we talk about how and where the pawns are positioned on the board we're talking about *pawn structure*.

Your pawn structure is the backbone of your position.

Unlike the pieces, which can make as many moves as they want in a single game, each pawn is only going to make six moves at most.

They're slow. They're weak. They can't go far.

And moving pawns isn't as important as moving pieces.

Because of this, most of your pawns are going to stay put for long stretches of the game.

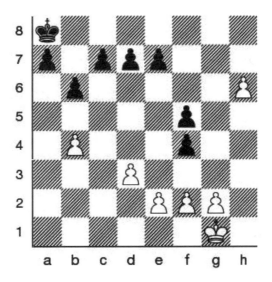

Figure 5-16

Here are some of the terms we use when we talk about pawn structure. Keep an eye on Figure 5-16.

Connected Pawns - When a pawn stands next to another pawn they are called *connected pawns*.

This is the best situation for them to be in.

Remember that pawns can't attack the square in front of them, but that's the only direction they can move! Because of this, they can get stuck really easily.

Two pawns standing side-to-side become both stronger and safer.

Here's an example of how connected pawns can work together:

The White pawns on **e2**, **f2** and **g2** are connected. So are the Black pawns on **c7**, **d7**, and **e7**.

If a White piece were to stand on square **c6**, the Black pawn on **c7** wouldn't be able to capture the piece. But the pawn on **d6** could.

Isolated Pawns - The other end of the coin is a pawn with no other pawn backing him up. This is called an *isolated pawn*.

Isolated pawns are very weak. They can attack, but not very well, and they have nobody to defend them.

Isolated pawns are just asking to be captured.

The White pawn on **b4** is an isolated pawn. He will never be able to move up the ranks.

The Black pawn on **b6** is *not* isolated.

Do you see why?

The pawns on **a7** and **c7** guard his square.

Doubled Pawns - When two pawns of the same color are on the same file together, they're called *doubled pawns*.

This is a bad position to be in.

Not only do doubled pawns have no way of protecting each other, but all it takes is for an enemy piece or pawn to step in front of them to make an instant traffic jam!

Then, both pawns are useless and neither one will be able to move forward.

The Black pawns on **f4** and **f5** are doubled pawns.

Passed Pawn - A pawn that has no enemy pawn in front of it, or on either file to its left or right side, is a *passed pawn*.

Watch out for these.

Why?

Because a passed pawn has a straight shot to a promotion! If he gets to the last rank, he'll be Queened.

The White pawn on **h6** is a passed pawn. Nothing's going to stop him from getting promoted.

The best structure - As you can see, you want to keep your pawns connected, and to get a passed pawn if you can.

Do your best to avoid positioning isolated and doubled pawns.

Putting it All Together

The best chess players know how to combine all of these tricks and ideas and use them in their games.

If you can become skilled at forking, pinning, double checking – even just at guarding or having a good pawn structure, you will be a fearsome player! And your opponents will be puppets at your command.

So study these techniques and think about them. As you play, be on the lookout for opportunities and possibilities to put them into use.

If chess is a dance, these moves are how you take the lead.

Chapter 6

Plan Ahead

I n 1999, the President of the United States of America, addressed the participants of a Chess World Championship with: "Chess is a game of strategy and concentration."

What President Clinton said was true, and both abilities are essential to winning chess. But there's also another important skill he didn't mention - tactics!

Let's look at what each of these words mean.

Concentration is the ability to focus.

It's important to pay attention to what happens in the game. Don't let yourself become distracted by noise or other things going on around you.

Strategy is a plan of action.

When you create a strategy, you set up a series of steps that you'll follow in order to accomplish a certain goal. It's the art of figuring out what needs to be done, and how you will best use your available resources to succeed.

Tactics are the specific actions you take, and reactions you make, as things happen.

In chess, tactics are based on where the pieces and pawns are positioned, and what one player expects the other player to do.

Much of what we learned in the last chapter – equal exchanges, pinning, forking, double checking and the discovered check – involve the skillful use of tactics.

In other words, tactics are about making *the right moves at the right time.*

Sure, chess players can win without concentrating on specific strategies. But if they don't apply good tactics based on each and every move, they won't win for very long.

The outcome of most chess games usually boils down to which player makes the best moves at the best times. Good tactics are crucial to winning chess!

This doesn't mean, however, that long-term strategy isn't just as important.

In fact, *a strategy should guide your tactics.*

Experience has shown that if you go into a chess match with a plan, no matter how much you have to change it later to fit your tactical needs, you'll have an advantage.

In other words, even a bad plan is better than no plan at all!

Seven Key Strategies

By now you know the goal of chess: to win by capturing the opponent's King, and to keep your own King safe.

Here you'll find a set of strategies used by the best chess players in the world, to help you reach your goals of winning, time and time again.

Learn them, use them, and you can't go wrong.

1. Control the Center

2. Make the Most of Your Moves

3. Keep Your King Safe

4. Build a Strong Pawn Structure

5. Be Mobile

6. Attack Wisely

7. Choose the Best Defense

Strategy #1 - Control the Center

The center of the board is the four middle squares: **d4**, **d5**, **e4** and **e5**. Controlling these squares is one of the most common, time-honored strategies in chess.

It's also one of the most important!

One of the early 20th century World Champions, Jose Capablanca, believed that in order to win, a player should control at least two squares in the center.

Why?

It's Where the Action Is – If you have control of the center of the board, your opponent will be forced to move along the sidelines.

This will not only cost your opponent extra moves, but will also result in your enemy's pieces getting in the way of each other.

United We Stand – It's important to keep your pieces as close together as possible, so that they can stay in a tight formation and work together.

The Heart of the Matter – The Kings rest on file **e** (at least in the beginning of the game), which is dead center in the board. Since the object of the game is to capture the enemy King and defend your own, it makes sense that you will want to focus most of your pieces where the Kings are.

Plus, it's easier to make attacks and defenses on the King, or on anyone else really, from the center since that's where your pieces can work together.

Piece Power – Think back on your pawn hunt with the Knight. Remember how much more he could do from the center?

It's not just him, though; *all* pieces are stronger and have more freedom of movement in the middle.

This is especially true of the weaker pieces (pawns, Knights and Bishops). They need the most help, so give them an advantage by putting them in the middle. Your Queen and Rooks can pick up the slack.

Strategy #2 - Make the Most of Your Moves

It doesn't matter whether or not you're using a chess clock to time your game, you should always think out each move as if you're under pressure.

Time is almost as important as material!

Be careful not to make a single unnecessary move. If you do, you're opening the door for your opponent to get into a better position.

A wasted move is like a wasted piece or pawn. This is truest during the first stage of the game, when you need to get your pieces out there (and in the center) as quickly as you can.

Before you make a move, any move, always ask yourself this question: "What does this move accomplish?"

If you can't answer that right away, think about it and don't make a move until you can!

Every move should do at least one of three things:

1. Threaten or capture something on your opponents side;

2. Defend something on your side; or

3. Put pressure on the center, or on your opponent's position.

In the next three chapters, we'll go into more detail about the three stages of a chess game and how to make the most of your moves during each one.

For now, just remember that making the best of each move is *essential* to winning.

Strategy #3 - Keep Your King Safe

Be aware of threats to your King *at all times* – both where they are and where they might be coming from – and be sure to take any steps necessary to protect him.

The King's Fortress – Remember this: In times of war, the first move should always be to protect those who are most important.

And that's what you need to do in the battle of chess: Protect your most important asset.

Castle your own King.

It's usually best to castle, and to do it as soon as you possibly can. It takes your King out of danger, and it also makes it easier to bring your Rook into play.

You want both of these things.

You can also castle on the Queen's side, but this means that you have to move your Queen out first. And that might not be a smart move – at least for a beginner.

Pawn Shield - Try to keep three pawns in front of your King at all times – one straight ahead and the other two at his diagonals. They will shield him from any potential attacks from your opponent's Bishop, Rook or Queen.

Strategy #4 - Build a Strong Pawn Structure

A good pawn structure is one in which the pawns work together; a bad pawn structure is one in which the pawns are working alone.

More than any other piece, the pawns need to help each other out, so keep your pawns as tightly linked as possible.

Here are a few tips for making a good pawn structure:

- Always have your pawns working in teams of two or more. Don't isolate them.
- Avoid doubling your pawns. A set of doubled pawns isn't worth much more than a single pawn.
- Remember to give your King a pawn shield.
- Keep a solid line of pawns across your territory to protect it, but never so that they block the ability of your pieces to move freely.

And while you're concentrating on strengthening your own pawn structure, don't forget to tear into your opponent's!

If you attack with your pieces, you'll force your opponent's to move forward. And if you capture enemy pawns, holes will appear in your opponent's line where your pieces can slide in and camp.

Strategy #5 - Be Mobile

A piece or pawn is no good to you if it's stuck.

A wise rule of thumb is this: The more mobile a piece, the stronger the piece. In other words, *mobility is power.*

Try to keep files open for your Rooks, diagonals for your Bishops and either or both for your Queen. How?

One smart way is to sacrifice, or better yet exchange, one of your pawns.

If getting rid of a pawn clears the way for one of your stronger pieces, do it! Yes you're losing material, but you're also getting a better position – and that's worth a lot.

If you see files or diagonals that are already open, quickly station your pieces so that you can control them. Remember, if you don't control that space, your opponent will!

If you have space under your control and room to move, you'll be on the road to victory.

Strategy #6 - Attack Wisely

By now I hope you've gotten the idea that when it comes to your army, they're all in this together.

Your pawns cover each other, your pieces guard and block enemy attacks and everyone protects the King.

Attacking the enemy position is done the same way.

Going After Pieces or Pawns - Whether you're gunning for the Queen, a Bishop or just a pawn, do it carefully! Capturing pieces or pawns can get you into trouble if you don't watch your step.

If you don't consider the consequences, many times a capture will leave you in a worse position than you were in before. So always stop, look and think.

Ask yourself:

- Is my attacking piece or pawn guarded by another one of my chess pieces? Are two or more pieces working together to make this capture?

- Is this capture going to weaken my position by opening up access holes to my more important pieces, or will it strengthen my position by taking space and material away from my opponent?

- Is my opponent setting up a trap by making this capture so easy for me?

- What will this capture do to help me win the game?

Remember, you don't win by taking your opponent's material. You win by checkmating the King.

Going for the King - Let's get one thing straight: A one-piece attack on other pieces or pawns is a bad idea, but a one-piece attack on the King is suicide!

Remember, to be checkmated the King has to be completely blocked off with no way to escape. Since he can move in any direction, this is trickier to pull off than you might think.

Checkmating almost always involves two or more pieces working together to create a solid barrier. Then, they attack the King from at least two different directions at once.

We'll get into details on checkmating in Chapter 9. But for now just keep in mind that your pieces will have to team up to take him down!

Strategy #7 - Choose the Best Defense

Every time an opponent's chess piece threatens one of yours, you're going to have to ask yourself a question with one of four possible answers:

Should I . . .

Capture it?
Block it?
Stay put?
or
Run away?

Capture it! - If the piece or pawn threatening you isn't protected, then you might just want to make the capture.

But think it through, because sometimes opponents will set up a sacrifice in order to trap you. Always look carefully when a capture seems too good to be true.

Block it! - Another easy way to stop a threat is to block the path between your piece and the one making the threat by putting another one of your chess pieces in the way.

For example, if the enemy Queen is threatening one of your Bishops and you have a pawn nearby, just move the pawn up to stand between the two.

Stay put! - Many times a threat isn't really a threat at all. It's often best just to leave things where they are, even when an enemy piece or pawn is threatening one of yours.

When two pieces are in each other's line of fire and both of them are guarded, there's no reason for either player to attack since neither one has an advantage. In situations like this, leave the empty threats alone and concentrate on something else.

Run away! - If one of your chess pieces is in trouble, has no protection, can't capture the threatening piece and you're not planning to sacrifice him for the sake of a plan, simply move him to a non-threatened square.

This is the simplest option of all – but it can also be the worst. You want to be pushing ahead, not retreating, for every move of the game.

It's always better to try and find a way of using a threat to your advantage than to just hide from it.

Don't be afraid to run if all else fails, but only run as a last resort!

The Seven Strategies in Action

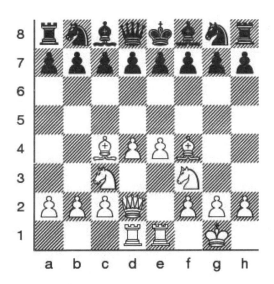

Figure 6-01

Imagine that you were playing as White, and that you could make your first ten moves of the game before Black made any at all.

Above is the "dream position" that you'd want to have. It would never happen in a real game, but it's worth looking at because it shows all seven of our key strategies working together.

Here's what I want you to notice:

Strategy #1: White completely owns the center of the board.

Not only do the pawns on **d4** and **e4** have 2 of the 4 center squares, but the **d** and **e** files are controlled by the Queen and two Rooks. All of the chess pieces are working together.

Strategy #2: White moved 9 chess pieces in 10 moves. Each piece and pawn, except for the King's Rook, moved only once.

You're in an unbeatable position – and in excellent time!

Strategy #3: The King was castled right away, and is safe behind a shield of pawns.

Strategy #4: The three pawns shielding the King on f, g and h are all connected, as are the two on d and e, so they can move forward with full support. Three more connected pawns sit on a, b and c, ready to attack and defend.

Strategy #5: Notice how all of White's pieces have either moved off the back rank or are free to move whenever they're ready. This army is going places!

Strategy #6: If White moved Ne5 and then Bxf7, we'd have an instant checkmate!

Of course, in a real game Black would be moving, but you can easily tell how strong White's position is. See how quickly an attack on the center turns into an attack on the King?

Strategy #7: The truth is that none of White's chess pieces are threatened right now – but even if any were, every single one of them is guarded.

The d and e pawns guard each other, and the Rooks and Queen act as backup for their files. The Knights protect the Bishops, the Queen and pawns protect the Knights, the pawns protect the King and so on.

The above example shows that using all seven strategies at once is possible. It's difficult, especially when Black is trying to get a good position too, but it can be done.

You should strive to keep all seven strategies going throughout the game. Succeed and you'll be unstoppable.

Chapter 7

Stage One: Send Out the Troops

Throughout the centuries, thousands of experts have contributed a lot of thoughts and ideas to the game of chess.

And even though most of the rules have stayed the same, players have invented many different ways to approach the game.

One of these approaches resulted in a system that divides a chess game into three separate stages: the *opening*, the *middle game* and the *endgame*.

All three stages are very different – and equally important. Entire books have been written about each one!

But since you're a beginner, I'll keep it simple. A chapter for each one will do for now.

What's the Opening?

The opening is the first few moves made on either side.

There is no strict definition as to exactly how many moves are involved in the opening, and there's no time limit. But that doesn't mean that time isn't important!

In fact, the opening is a race.·

The winner is the player who can get their pieces out from behind the pawns and into a good position first. This is called *developing* your pieces.

One good way to think of development is the movement of the troops to the frontier line, which is the line between each player's half of the board.

Past that line is enemy territory.

Opening Objectives

You've got a mission to accomplish in the opening.

These are your two main goals:

• To move your pieces into a strong defensive line for your King, as well as a strong attack position toward your opponent's King; and

• To gain at least some control of the center of the board.

Remember that the effect of every move you and the other player makes in the opening is going to ripple into the future of the game.

The choices you make here are investments – just like saving money for hard times.

Opening Tips and Tactics

Start with a Pawn

The first move you make in the game should be the Queen or King's pawn (**d** or **e**).

Why?

Because it gets a pawn into the center of the board right away, and also frees up one of your Bishops to move out.

As you know, a pawn can move one or two squares in its first move, to rank 3 or 4. For now, go for 4.

Moving a pawn to **d4** or **e4** is the most common first chess move in the world.

So why not do what successful people do? If **e4** is good enough for world champions, it'll work for you too.

But even though it's valuable and important to make a few pawn moves, they aren't considered developing moves. The pawns are mostly just clearing the way for your other pieces to develop.

Keep in mind, though, that once a pawn moves forward, he can never go back. Move pawns only if you've already mapped out a strategy.

Get Them All Out of Bed

Your pieces are anxious; they're chomping at the bit to come out from behind the pawns.

You need what's called *piece activity*. Good piece activity is making sure that everybody is equally involved and doing their part for the team.

Each piece should go out, one after the other. Don't let *anyone* fall behind!

Knights before Bishops

After the pawn, the Knight should be the first piece you move.

Remember that he can jump over other chess pieces, so you don't need to move your Knight's pawn out of his way.

Why should you move the Knights before Bishops?

Again, think back to what you learned by playing the Knight pawn hunt game: A Knight on the rim is dim!

Bishops are better in the center of the board too, but they can work from a distance. So it's more important to get your Knights out there right away.

A good second move if you're playing White would be to move your Queen's Knight to c3 or your King's Knight to f3; if you're playing Black, move your Queen's Knight to c6 or your King's Knight to f6.

After that, you might move your other Knight. Or, you can go ahead and send out your King's Bishop.

Where do I put my Bishops?

The White King's Bishop (he starts on f1) could go to b5, c4, d3 or e2.

The move you decide upon depends on what your opponent is up to.

While you're moving your pawns and Knights, keep an eye on his army. By that time you should have an idea as to where your Bishops should move.

Protect the Royalty

Your moves so far have been leading up to something.

Not only have you gotten some hold of the center and have begun to threaten the other side, there's now a clear path between your King and Rook.

Castle him now!

And then protect your Queen as well.

She is much more effective later in the game, after there have been some captures and exchanges – so keep her safe by not bringing her out too early.

Plus, if you lose the Queen too soon, you've taken a huge step toward losing the game.

Rooks Can Chill Out

It's not so important to get your Rooks moving as it is to find good spots for your Knights, Bishops and a few pawns.

If you've castled, the Rook you used is already in a good place because he's controlling a file close to the center. He's fine for now and so is the Queen's Rook.

That's all the development you need.

However, if you feel like you've got time, go ahead and move your Queen up to the second rank and put her Rook on file **d**.

Getting the Rooks into the game is all about timing; it's important to know when to use them. And as you gain experience you'll develop a better feel for the best time to get your Rooks out onto the battlefield.

One Man, One Move

Once you have moved a piece or pawn, leave it where it is until all of your pieces have been moved. Only move a piece or pawn twice if it becomes threatened and you want to save it from capture.

Like I said, the opening is a race to see who can get themselves into position first. Moving a piece twice is just wasting moves, and therefore time.

Be decisive! Your pieces want clear orders.

Pick the best square for each one, and have them each stay put until they're needed for something else.

Ahead of the Game

If you notice that your opponent is wasting moves, do something about it!

Threaten his or her position by opening up lines for your better pieces.

On the other hand, if you're behind in development, keep your lines closed off until you can catch up.

Know Your Role

In the opening you'll have a different goal depending on whether you're playing as Black or as White.

White has a slight advantage because he moves first. In a way, that decides what Black needs to do on his first move.

If you're White, your goal is to keep that going! Make strong, aggressive moves to force Black into playing defensively.

If you're playing as Black, make bold moves of your own. Scare White into playing your game, by your rules.

In the beginning, White's goal is to get a foothold, while Black's goal is to keep things equal by either weakening that foothold or setting up one of his own that's just as strong.

Give and Take

When it comes to captures and exchanges, the rule is to keep it to a minimum. The opening is a time to set up your forces, not to attack.

Remember our seven strategies. It's not wise to pick a fight until all the pieces are developed and working together.

But there are times when you might want to sacrifice or exchange a piece or pawn.

Do it if:

- It will give you a big advantage in development;
- It deflects your opponent's Queen, or lures her out into the open;
- It prevents your opponent from castling; or
- It enables a strong attack to be developed.

Quick Tips

- Remember that poor placement of even a single piece can destroy the relationship of the other pieces. Make sure they're all in the best possible position.
- Don't move pawns without carefully planning a strategy first.
- Unless it will get your pieces into a *much* better position, never allow your pawn structure to be weakened.
- Don't be eager to grab material in the opening. The fight for time is much more important than the battle for pieces.
- Don't make aimless moves. Each move should be related to the development of the game, and hopefully part of a bigger plan.
- If you lose your hold on the center, try to get back in there with a backup piece.
- Even if you see pawns that look like they're just begging to be captured, there is no time for pawn hunting in the opening of the game. Instead, keep your focus on developing; it will be much better in the long run.

The Game is on!

It should take between 8 and 10 moves to develop your pieces.

An example of a good opening development would be:

1. A center pawn

2. The King's Knight

3. The Queen's Knight

4. The King's Bishop

5. (castle)

6. Another center pawn

7. The Queen's Bishop

8. The King's Rook or another pawn or a capture

If you can do this or something like it, you're probably in good shape and ready for an exciting middle game.

The last word on the opening is this: *Keep it tight and keep it simple.*

Break it down, and that's the essence of what all the great chess masters do.

Experiment with and memorize several different openings so that you'll have some flexibility for any situation that might arise.

But be sure to know at least one opening very well. A good, solid idea of openings builds up your confidence for the rest of the game.

A Chess Game in Action: The Opening

Let's go back to the game between me and Rashid that you followed in Chapter 3.

But this time, instead of studying the chess notation, let's take a close look at *why* the moves were made by peeking inside the minds of the players.

Again, use a chess set if you have one. Otherwise, follow along with the pictures.

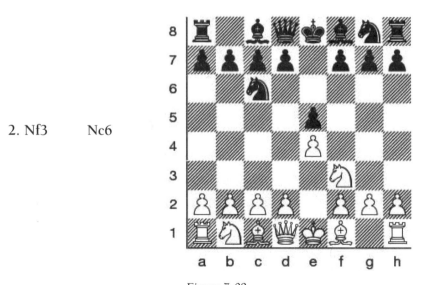

1. e4   e5

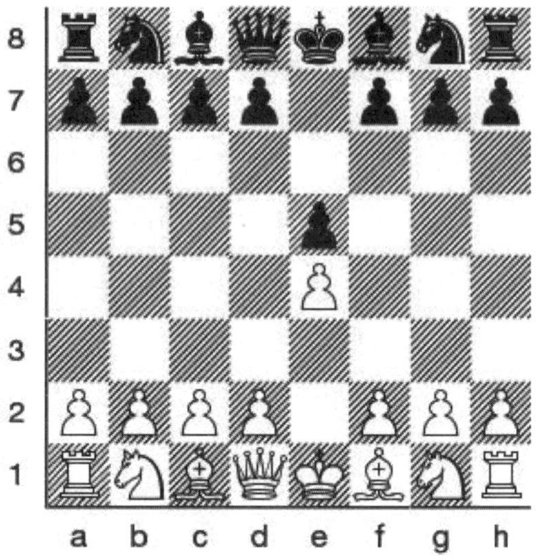

Figure 7-01

Simple as it gets.

I move my King's pawn to **e4** and Rashid responds by putting his King's pawn directly in front of it. Both pawns are now blockading each other.

These moves also free both of our King's Bishops to move out.

2. Nf3   Nc6

Figure 7-02

Several things have just happened.

First of all, by placing my King's Knight on f3, I'm now threatening Rashid's pawn on e5. He then immediately moves to guard the pawn by placing his Queen's Knight on c6.

This way, if I capture his pawn, he can take my Knight in retaliation.

At the same time, the move develops both of our Knights and places them near the center of the board.

Two moves to each of us, and there's already been a threat and a defense! The game's exciting already.

3. Bc4   Bc5

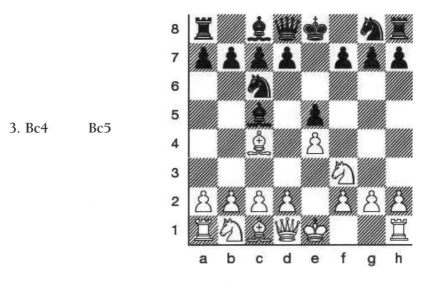

Figure 7-03

These Bishop moves are mainly just for development. But the move is effective in helping both of us put pressure on each other's positions.

I am threatening f7; he is threatening f2. Right now these are the weakest squares on the board because they're only protected by our Kings.

Do you see my other possible Bishop move?

I could have made an aggressive attack on his **c6** Knight by putting my Bishop on **b5**.

So why didn't I?

It was just my favorite choice. Lots of grand masters will play **Bb5** but for me, putting pressure on **f7** is good enough for now.

4. Nc3   Nf6

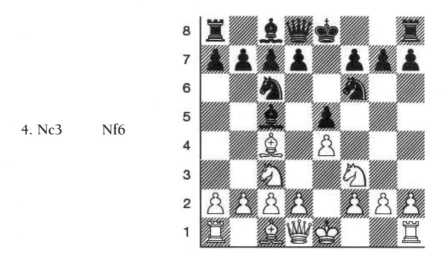

Figure 7-04

Here's the mirror image of our second moves. This time it's his Knight that's come out to threaten my pawn, and my Knight swooping in to defend.

Now all of the Knights are developed.

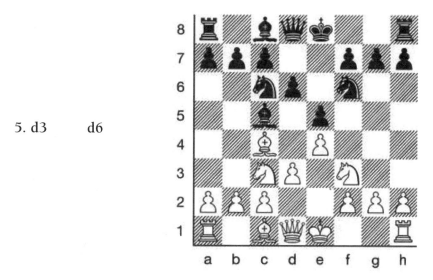

5. d3   d6

Figure 7-05

Moving out our **d** pawns frees up our Queen's Bishops. It also puts a little more pressure on the center.

But do you see why neither of us was able to move our pawn up two squares?

Because it would have been pawn suicide! Squares **d4** and **d5** are dangerous right now, each one controlled by both an enemy Bishop and an enemy pawn.

At this point the board is exactly the same on both sides and neither of us has a positional advantage. All we've done is match each other, move for move.

And if you're wondering why neither of us has castled yet, even though the way has been open for two rounds, this is why:

Until one of us has some kind of advantage in time, position or material, we have to keep up with each other's development. Otherwise the one who stops to castle would fall behind.

6. Be3   Bg4

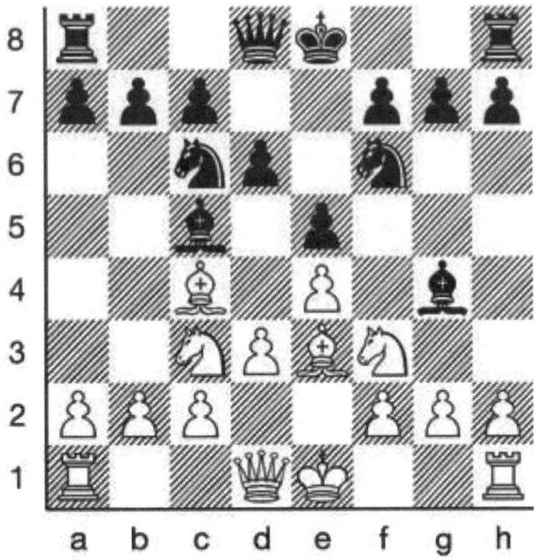

Figure 7-06

Now our development is finally finished and Rashid and I are both ready to start breaking off into our own plans.

The opening is done!

Rather than put my Bishop out on **g5**, I've decided to keep him close to home on **e3** to guard my territory (moving to **f4** or **h6** would just lead to a capture by one of Rashid's pawns).

Did you notice that my e3 Bishop and Rashid's c5 Bishop are threatening each other, and that both are protected by pawns? There's not going to be any action there.

But what is Rashid up to? He's now threatening my f3 Knight with his other Bishop.

Is he going to take my Knight? And if so, why, with my **g2** pawn standing guard?

Find out what Rashid's thinking when the game continues at the end of the next chapter.

Chapter 8

Stage Two: The Heat of Battle

The game is on. You and your opponent have developed your pieces, set up individual game plans and maybe have two or three captures under your belt.

Your strategies are starting to take shape and the stage is set for a major attack.

You are now in middle game.

What is Middle Game?

Middle game is the point in a chess game when the soldiers of both armies start battling it out by capturing each other and moving forward through enemy lines.

Like I said earlier, there's no specific marker or move that lets you know when you've reached middle game – but you'll know once you're there.

If each player's pieces are developed, or are nearly developed, and the game is getting more aggressive – or even more interesting – then you're in middle game.

Middle Game Objectives

Unlike the opening, there is no clear or specific goal to middle game. It's more about coming up with plans (strategies) and carrying them out (tactics) based on what has happened so far.

You're really going to have to start using your head at this point in the game!

A lot of times you can get through the opening just by playing through a series of moves you've done a hundred times before – especially if your opponent is playing along with a standard opening.

But now, at middle game, you'll need to think things through and be more creative.

The opening can be very routine, like getting ready to go to school. You wake up, get dressed, brush your teeth, have breakfast and get on the bus.

You may have to do things a little differently from time to time, but usually it's just about doing the same thing every day.

Arriving at middle game is like sitting down in class. Now you've got to turn on your brain and apply yourself to the problems and tasks ahead.

It's tough, but if you apply yourself and pay attention, you'll succeed.

Middle Game Tips and Tactics

Develop or Die!

If your opponent has all of his pieces out and ready but you don't, your first task is to finish your development as quickly as you can.

Otherwise, you might find yourself under attack and unprepared to make a defense!

If you've worked quickly in the opening then this shouldn't be a problem. But if you made some early captures you might be a little behind.

It's time to make up for lost time.

Get Your Rooks in the Game

In the opening, the Rooks didn't see much action. The middle game is when you want to bring them into focus.

If you can, get your own chess pieces out of the way and clear files for them to control. Remember that Strategy #5 is to stay mobile.

Also remember that you might have to sacrifice or exchange a pawn to do it. Don't be afraid to sacrifice a pawn if it will put your Rooks into a good position.

Keep in mind that Rooks can cross the entire board in one move, so it's best to keep them on the back rank, safe in your territory, until you're ready to attack.

Blockaded Bishops

Many times one of your Bishops will have been captured or exchanged late in the opening or early in the middle game.

If this happens, make your remaining Bishop more effective by keeping squares of his designated color clear.

If he's your dark square Bishop, make sure your army isn't blocking too many dark squares; if he's your light square Bishop, keep your light squares clear.

Mobility, after all, is power!

When it comes to your opponent's Bishops, keep them blockaded by shoving pawns in the way.

The Knights: Location, Location, Location!

If you've put your Knights out into the c and f files, good job. Now the trick is to keep them there.

Unless there's something you need to attack or defend, your Knights should be standing guard at the center of the board. Don't put them on the edges!

I've already mentioned one reason for this several times (his range of movement is better in the center), but there's also another reason: The closer your Knight is to the center, the closer he is to each and every spot on the board.

That way, if he's needed somewhere, he can get there much faster.

Lady in Waiting

Middle game strategy for the Queen is simple: Keep her out of danger and near the King where she can protect him.

Move her out only if you see an important capture that won't put her at risk.

The idea is to keep the Queen safe until the endgame, when she will be the most valuable to you.

Cramping Your Style

Depending on how the opening unfolded, you might find yourself getting cramped. Maybe you've got too many blockaded pieces and not a whole lot of options for moving them.

You need to get yourself mobile.

The best way to do that is to exchange some of your pawns and maybe a few pieces. But try and keep it equal!

Let's say your Bishop is stuck on a diagonal and blocked off by an enemy Knight or Bishop. Take that piece, even if it means that an enemy pawn can take your Bishop on the next move.

You can't be afraid to exchange a piece if it's going to help your game overall!

And if it's your opponent who's cramped?

The best thing you can do is keep it that way.

You might see him or her making an attempt to exchange pieces or pawns and if so, don't let it happen! If you're open and your opponent's stuck, go on the attack.

Don't Pick Fights

If you're attacking and you've got three or more pieces that are working together (which is the best way to attack, I might add) try to avoid exchanging pieces with your opponent.

Keep bearing down on that King! If you start in with one-on-one battles, you're going to lose focus on your attack and your pieces are going to lose communication with each other.

Keep your pieces talking and keep them unified! Always look at the game three to four moves ahead.

Scattered Pawns

Remember Strategy #4: A strong pawn structure is important.

If your opponent has weakened his structure during the opening, or if any of his pawns are doubled, then go after the pawns!

This will force your opponent to defend pawns with other pieces, and you'll tip the scales heavily against him.

Look for any space between two pawns. If you see a file that's open, try and get your Rook over there right away so that you can take control of the file.

Then, even better, send a Bishop or a Knight to the other end of the same file.

That way you'll be deep into your opponent's territory and you'll have a Rook backing up your piece, ready to attack anyone who takes it. There will be no way for your opponent to get your piece out of there without losing time, material or both.

In the meantime, don't forget to keep your own pawn structure strong to keep your challenger from doing the same thing to you.

Any space between two of your pawns might open up an opportunity for the other player to take over a file, or to post a Bishop or Knight in your territory.

Give and Take

If you are ahead by one or more pieces, exchange as many pieces as you can!

Just think of this: *The fewer the pieces there are on the board, the more powerful all the remaining pieces become.*

Less enemy pieces on the board mean fewer threats to your pawns. And fewer threats equal a greater chance that one or more of those pawns will make it to the eighth rank for a promotion.

To keep it simple, remember this advice:

If you are ...

- Ahead in pieces or

- Even in pieces, but ahead in pawns

... then exchange pieces!

If you are ...

- Behind in pieces, but ahead in pawns

... then exchange pawns!

If you are ...

- Behind in pieces and pawns

... don't exchange anything!

Balancing Act

If you're concentrating your attacks on one side of the board, be sure that your other side isn't vulnerable to an attack by your opponent.

Make a move or two to protect yourself.

If you're getting heavily attacked on one side, the best thing to do is attack on the opposite side (or the center). Your opponent will then have to bring back some of his pieces to defend himself.

Quick Tips

- The middle game is the time to take risks. Don't be afraid to make daring, aggressive moves.

- Always remember to protect your King. One of the biggest mistakes many players make during the middle game is to focus so much on attacking their opponent that they forget to look after their own.

- Try to stay in teams, both for attack and defense. Two pieces working together are twice as good as one piece on its own; they can help each other in many ways.

A Chess Game in Action: Middle Game

Let's get back to the game, right where we left off in Chapter 7.

If your chess pieces are still in place, then great. If not, set them up so that they match Figure 7-06:

7. Qd2   Bxf3

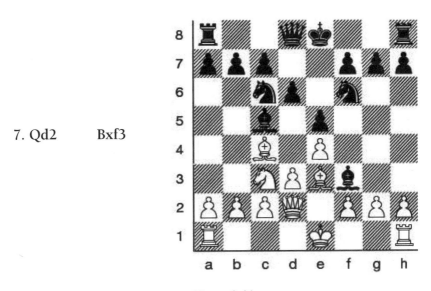

Figure 8-01

I've just moved my Queen up one square. This is to clear off the first rank so that I can make a Queen's side castle.

Why a Queen's side?

Because I've looked a few moves ahead. I can already see that my position on the King's side is about to become weaker.

Plus, I think there might be some fighting there soon, which makes it a bad place for the King to be.

Sure enough, on the very next move, Rashid makes the first capture of the game by taking my Knight on f3!

But that's no problem, because now his Bishop is threatened by my g2 pawn.

8. gxf3   Nd4

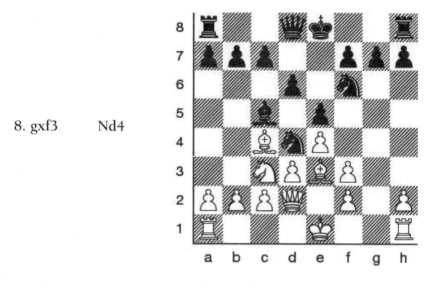

Figure 8-02

Taking Rashid's Bishop here is, really, my only choice.

First, I need to even out the loss of my Knight. He was worth 3 points and Rashid's Bishop is also worth 3, making it an equal exchange.

Second, the Bishop and my g pawn are both threatening each other, so it's either him or me! Though this capture gives me doubled pawns on the f file and hurts my pawn structure, I'm going to do it.

It's not the best choice, but I can also turn this disadvantage into an advantage. Yes I have doubled pawns, but now the g file is an open line into Rashid's territory.

Keep this sort of thing in mind when you're playing. Let the seven strategies be a guide, not hard, fast rules.

If weakening your pawn structure, sacrificing material or even leaving your King open to attack is going to help you accomplish something big, be flexible and go for it.

Knowing when and how to loosen up on strategy is what makes a good chess player.

Rashid's next move is to come in with his Knight and threaten my f3 pawn.

But see how by putting his Knight there, he is opening himself up to be captured by my Bishop?

9. Bxd4   Bxd4

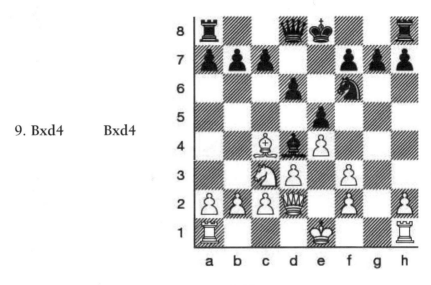

Figure 8-03

I decide to capture Rashid's Knight with my Bishop, who is then captured right back by Rashid's Bishop!

Now we've each lost one Knight and one Bishop, making us still even in material.

This is definitely a tight game!

10. 0-0-0   c6

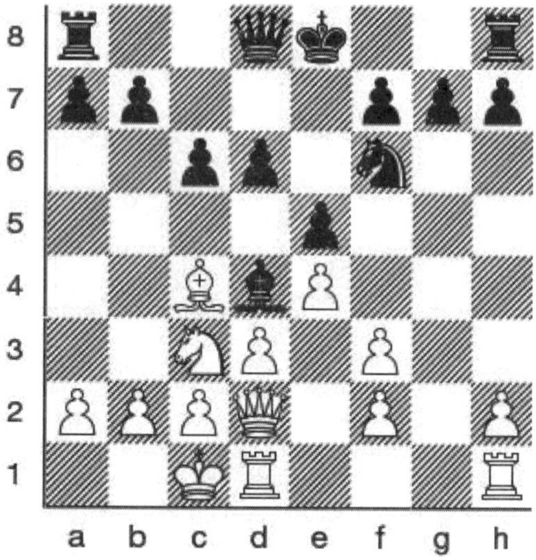

Figure 8-04

Now that all of my chess pieces are safe and the game is balanced, I finally have time to castle.

Castling isn't always done in the opening, and this game is a good example of when and why it sometimes doesn't happen right away. Do you understand why I had to wait until now?

Also, look at the King's side of the board. Do you see why castling there would be a bad idea?

It's a very poor place for him, because there's nothing there to protect him but a few scattered pawns.

On the other hand, the Queen's side offers a pawn shield, a Knight and a Bishop in the area – and the Queen herself is protecting the diagonal that the King will be castled to!

I couldn't ask for anything more.

As for Rashid, he has decided to set off on a more aggressive strategy.

Instead of castling or taking my Knight with his Bishop (my Knight is guarded by my Queen), he's advancing a pawn. He wants to start a forward movement of his troops into my territory, to force me into playing defensively.

But why did he move his pawn only one square? You'll understand on his next move.

11. R(h)g1   b5

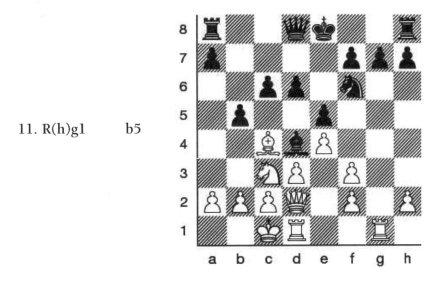

Figure 8-05

Next I move my King's Rook over one square.

This is an open file, so I can control it. I also suspect that Rashid might castle King's-side, which would put him on the **g** file, straight across from my Rook.

Rashid moves another pawn forward to threaten my Bishop.

I could take that pawn with my Bishop or my Knight, but that would be a mistake. His **b5** pawn is guarded by his **c6** pawn.

Now do you see why he moved his pawn to **c6** instead of **c5**? It's because he planned ahead for this move, to set up protection for his **b5** pawn.

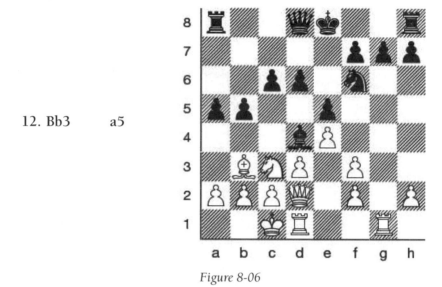

12. Bb3   a5

Figure 8-06

The way in which Rashid protects his **b5** pawn forces my Bishop into a retreat. To make matters worse, Rashid then moves his **a3** pawn up two squares.

That puts a lot of pressure on my position.

Almost all of my Queen's-side pieces and pawns are stuck now! I need to clear some space for them to move.

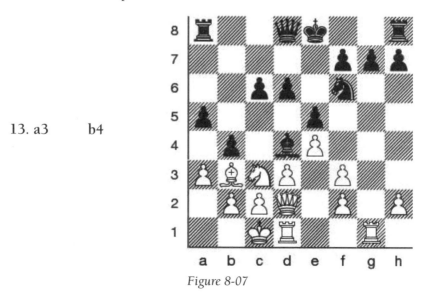

13. a3   b4

Figure 8-07

Now I move my **a** pawn out, hoping that Rashid will set me up for a pawn exchange.

Like I said, I need space, so getting a couple pawns off the board is necessary.

Rashid plays right along.

He wants an exchange too, but for his own reasons. His goal is to clear space on the **a** file for his Rook.

14. axb4   axb4

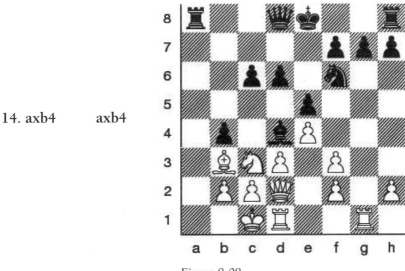

Figure 8-08

There it is - I take his pawn, he takes mine. We're both still equal in material, but this changes everything in terms of position.

I have a few more options for movement now, but a critical hole has just opened up in my position. Do you see it?

If Rashid can manage to take my Knight on **c3** with his **b4** pawn or **d4** Bishop, and then move his Queen's Rook from **a8** to **a1**, the game will be over. Instant checkmate!

Will I notice it in time?

15. Nb1   0-0

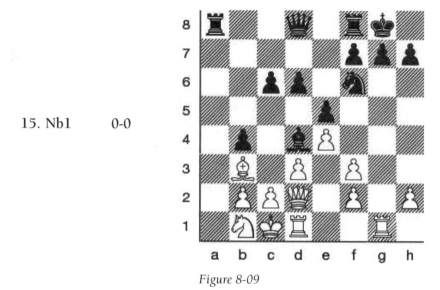

Figure 8-09

Luckily I do see the threat. This is a game-saving move for me; if I hadn't made it, I would have lost.

But moving my Knight to **b1** does a lot more than remove him from the double-threat of Rashid's pawn and Bishop. More importantly, it keeps his Rook from swooping in and attacking my King.

For now, I'm safe.

Rashid takes this opportunity to make a King's-side castle.

His Queen hasn't moved out yet, so a Queen's-side castle is impossible. Moving her out would cause him to fall behind in time, and Queen's-side wouldn't be a good place for his King anyway.

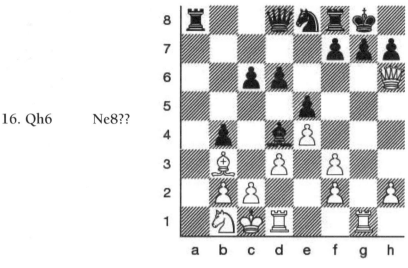

16. Qh6   Ne8??

Figure 8-10

With one move, everything has changed.

Rashid is in big trouble now; my Queen has just come in for the kill.

She's safe from the pawn on **g7**, since that capture would put Rashid's King into check by my Rook on **g1** (remember the rule: you can't make a move that puts your own King into check). Rashid has no choice but to leave the Queen there, breathing down his neck.

Rashid is desperate. He moves his Knight back to **e8**, in order to guard the **g7** pawn from capture.

But this is a mistake. Instead, he actually should have moved that pawn one space forward by playing **g6**.

Why?

Because it would have made it impossible for my Queen to attack. If she moved to **g7** it would be a check, but his King could just capture her, and his **g6** pawn would shield him from my **g1** Rook.

Unfortunately, Rashid made the wrong move – and it just about seals his fate.

17. Rxg7!!   Nxg7

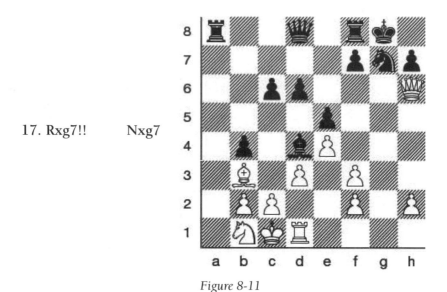

Figure 8-11

Now my Rook comes forward to take the pawn from **g7** and put the King in check.

I know that Rashid's reply will be to take my Rook with his Knight, but it's a sacrifice I'm willing to make.

18. Rg1   *resigns*

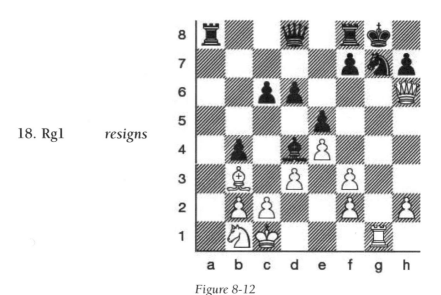

Figure 8-12

Now I simply move my remaining Rook over to the **g** file. It doesn't matter what Rashid does now; I will win.

This is because:

- He can't move his Knight, since it would put his King into check. (An illegal move!)
- There's no use moving any other piece, because Rashid knows that my next move is going to be **Qxg7**, whether he likes it or not. And if I move there, he has no more options.
- Once I move **Qxg7**, he won't be able to capture my Queen with his King. It's a checkmate no matter what, since my Rook is at the other end of the file.

Do you see any more options?

If you said "move **Qg5**," good eye, but in that case, I'd just move **Rxg5**. I'd be a move behind, but it wouldn't matter, since none of Rashid's other pieces would be able to get there in time to stop me from moving **Qxg7** and trapping him.

But What about the Endgame?

Surprise! This one is over.

That's right; Rashid and I didn't even make it to the endgame. It happens.

Some games can end with a checkmate during the opening, in as little as four moves!

There was no checkmate either. Rashid resigned because he knew he was beaten.

And that's why I showed you this game – to make the point that neither an endgame nor a forced checkmate will always, definitely happen.

But remember what I told you in Chapter 2: Don't ever resign! Leave that to the professionals.

Why?

For one thing, it's just good practice to play to the end. But also because there's a strong chance that, even if you're in a position as bad as Rashid's, a less experienced player won't see what you do.

He might not realize that he's got you trapped, even if you realize it. Then he'll make the wrong move and you can use that chance to get yourself to safety.

The bottom line is that you need many years of experience under your belt before you even start thinking about resigning.

Let's move on now to the final stage of chess: the endgame.

Chapter 9

Stage Three: The Big Win

The battle has been waged; the armies are tired. There are only a few pieces and pawns left on each side.

Sometimes one player will have a big advantage; other times the scales will be nearly balanced.

This is the time when a single good move can bring you victory, and a tiny mistake can just as easily bring it all crashing down.

Welcome to endgame.

What is Endgame?

Endgame is the exciting final stage of a chess battle, when you and your opponent try to force each other into checkmate.

Like the opening and middle game, there's no definite sign telling you when you've passed into endgame. But you might notice that the board is starting to look a little deserted, like a party that's breaking up.

If most of the chess pieces are gone and you and your opponent are focusing on nothing more than trying to pin down each other's Kings, you'll know you're in endgame.

The Objective

You only have one real goal in endgame – get that King!

Hopefully you're ahead in material, but if not, just a couple of pieces may be enough for you to win if you play it smart.

What's New?

The biggest difference between endgame and everything that came before is that now the pawns and the King can serve as strong attacking weapons.

Attacking with the King

Once most or all of the big pieces have been taken off of the board, the King is in less danger and has more maneuverability.

It's time to get him moving. Try and work him into the center, or into your opponent's side of the board.

Just keep him away from the edges! A King stuck in the corner is, as you'll see later, one of the surest paths to a checkmate.

If you have any pieces left, be sure to keep them close to the King. Not only will it support your King, but it will make it easier for your army to work together for a final attack.

Pawn Potential

If you have a passed pawn, concentrate on getting him to the last rank for a promotion. Give him support and protection with your other pawns or pieces, and make it as hard as possible for your opponent to blockade or capture him.

Making a run to promote one of your pawns is an important part of many endgames – but it's not always a good idea.

Odds are that it'll take too many moves to get him to the last rank. And besides, you'll probably have bigger problems to take care of.

Go for it only if you have the time and a good position.

Meanwhile, pay attention to your opponent to make sure he's not trying to promote one of his own pawns.

Rooks in the Endgame

If you still have one or both of your Rooks, get them behind your passed pawns as protection.

If you still have both of your Rooks, try putting them as deep as you can into enemy territory – rank 7 if you're playing as White or rank 2 if you're playing as Black.

Aside from the Queen, the Rooks are the most powerful checkmating weapon you have.

Give and Take

If you're behind, hold on to your pieces at all costs!

But if you're still ahead by a piece or two, keep exchanging – just like you were doing in middle game. That one extra piece is usually all you need to win.

If you can get rid of your opponent's pawns, it will lower his chances of promoting and also make it harder for him to corner your King.

Keep Your Eye on the Prize

I once lost to a State champion, in a game that I felt I'd played well. Afterward, I asked my opponent for his opinion and he explained what I'd done wrong:

"Orrin, you had everything you needed to win. But you lost the game because you got greedy. You made captures you didn't need."

Looking back, I could see that he was right.

The number of chess pieces you capture doesn't matter in the end!

A player's chess army has only one purpose – to protect its own King. You capture pieces and pawns to make your opponent's King weaker and more vulnerable.

You don't capture chess pieces for points, to collect as trophies or to use as bragging rights.

Don't go after pieces or pawns if you don't have a good reason.

It's an important lesson that every chess player needs to learn.

Because every move you waste trying to take material is one more chance for your opponent to come from behind with a surprise win. Don't let it happen.

Keep your eye on the prize. Go for the game and get that King!

Piece Power

In the endgame, it's all about the power of the pieces.

Bishops have a lot of power on the diagonals. And if there are a lot of pawns on the board, Knights become more of an advantage since they'll have no problem jumping over a line of pawns.

But what you really want in endgame is at least one Rook or, even better, a Queen.

Match them up with any other piece and you'll have a far better chance than with just Bishops or Knights.

Look for a Checkmate!

Every player needs to have an idea of checkmates and how they work.

A checkmate usually doesn't just happen; it's forced when two or more chess pieces work together to trap the enemy King.

You have to plan for it, and set it up several moves in advance.

Unless you know how checkmates work, you might not know what to do, even if you have everything you need to win.

There's a chance, though, that a checkmate might happen naturally. Your opponent might fall into it by accident, or you could manage to work it out a move at a time until it clicks into place.

But that's letting the game control you, and I want *you* to control the game!

All about Checkmates

So this is it. Last but not least, the final major chess lesson you need to learn: Checkmates.

In the old days, when Kings were kept safe inside the fortress of their castle walls, the enemy had to be creative in finding ways of breaking through the outside defenses.

One effective tool was the battering ram.

Attackers would cut down a tree, march to the castle and pound against the doors until they were smashed open. Then, the troops would rush through to storm the castle.

Nobody inside, including the King, had anywhere to run. They were forced to fight off the invaders – and if they failed, they would lose the castle.

I want you to think of checkmating in the same way: Smash through the defenses, trap the enemy and corner the King!

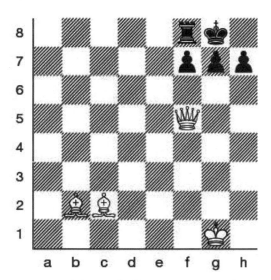

Figure 9-1: It's Black's turn to move. What would you do?

In the above diagram, White's Bishops and Queen are acting like one of these old-style battering rams.

If it were White's turn to move, the Queen could move to the **h7** square, break a hole in the wall by capturing the pawn and checkmate the King right then and there.

What could Black do to prevent this?

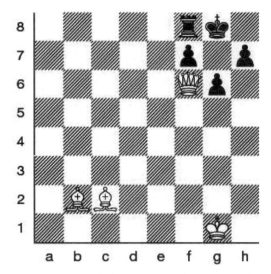

Figure 9-2: Black moves g6; White moves Qf6.

In this example, Black sees the **Qxh7** threat. But instead of bringing out his Rook to threaten the Bishops and give his King room to escape, he pushes his **g** pawn forward to threaten White's Queen and to block her from moving **Qxh7**.

This isn't the right choice. Now Black's King is going to be check-mated, and there's nothing he can do.

White can't get the **Qxh7** checkmate now, but it makes no differ-ence. She just moves forward one space to **Qf6**.

Now she's all set for her last move.

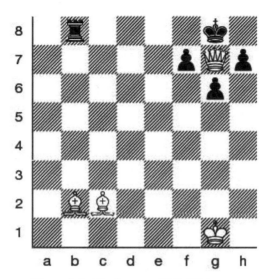

*Figure 9-3: Black moves **Rb8**; White moves Qg7.*

Now it's Black's turn. He moves his Rook out to threaten White's Bishop but it's too late.

White moves to **Qg7**.

Checkmate!

Here's how:

- The White Queen checks the Black King, but the King can't escape to f8 or h8 because the White Queen controls those squares.

- The Black King can't escape to **f7** or **h7** because his own pawns are in the way (plus, the White Queen controls those squares too).

- None of Black's chess pieces can block the White Queen's attack.

- The Black King can't move forward one square and capture the White Queen because he'd then be in check by the White Bishop on **b2**.

- The Black Rook can't take the White Bishop on **b2** because that move wouldn't get his King out of check. (Remember, it is illegal to make a move that leaves a King in check.)

Steps to a Checkmate

The last example showed a few important ideas and techniques.

But for a surefire win, these are some of the ways in which you can make a checkmate:

1. **Judge the position by whose turn it is.**

   Remember that in *Figure 9-1* White could have checkmated in one move (**Qxh7**) if it were White's turn. But it was Black's turn, and that made all the difference.

   Judging any board position depends on who is next to move. It's especially important in the last few moves of a game.

2. **Make a hole in your opponent's pawn formation.**

   Attacking your challenger's pawn formation will weaken his King's defense. By moving your pieces around, you can take full advantage of the hole you created.

   Again, see *Figure 9-1*: White's Queen scared Black's g7 pawn into moving forward.

3. **Use mistakes by the other player to your advantage.**

   If Black had moved his Rook out to threaten the Bishops, the whole game would have gone in a different direction.

   When you're waiting for your opponent to make a move, always try to think to yourself what he or she *should* do, and why. And if they make a mistake, be ready to make them pay for it!

4. **Set up a barrier against the King.**

   See *Figure 9-2*: White's Bishops are acting as a very powerful barrier. With the diagonals they control, the King has nowhere to escape!

5. **Deliver the checkmate with another piece.**

   See *Figure 9-3*. With support from the Bishop, the Queen checkmates on g7.

The Basic Checkmates

In the last example, White had his Queen plus two Bishops – and that's more than enough material to force a checkmate.

Black had his Rook and a few pawns for attack and defense.

But what if it comes down to just a few pieces? What's the bare minimum you need in order to force the other player into checkmate?

And if it comes down to the bare minimum, what exactly do you have to do?

These are all important questions. To answer them, chess players study a set of patterns known as the *basic checkmates.*

There are five basic checkmates. Each one is a combination of two or more pieces working together against a defenseless King, after the rest of his army has been captured.

1. Two Rooks vs. King
2. Rook and King vs. King
3. Queen and King vs. King
4. Two Bishops and King vs. King
5. Bishop, Knight and King vs. King

Checkmate *cannot* be forced with only:

1. One Knight (or even two Knights) and the King
2. One Bishop and the King
3. The King alone

If the situation is that bad, the enemy King will almost never be checkmated because unless the other player makes a mistake, the King will always have an escape square.

If this is all you have left, hopefully you'll have a pawn to promote. Otherwise you and your opponent will have to agree to a draw.

Why Study the Basic Checkmates?

While you go through the next section, you should have your board and pieces out, following along.

It's important to practice these checkmates because they'll teach you how to win in a "basic checkmate" endgame.

Plus:

- **You'll learn how checkmates look and "feel."**

  Capturing a piece is easy and straightforward, but checkmating a King is trickier than you might think – especially if you've never done it. You can't really understand checkmates until you gain some experience.

- **Your ability to visualize will improve.**

  Remember how important visualization is in chess? You need to look ahead, to see things and plan them before they happen. Working out the basic checkmates is a great way to get better at this essential skill.

- **You'll learn to checkmate in as few moves as possible.**

  In Chapter 2 I talked about the "50 Moves Rule," in which a game ends in a draw if 50 moves go by without any captures. If you just chase the other King around you'll use up your 50 moves and you won't win! Study the basic checkmates and you'll know how to finish him off quickly.

Strategy of the Basic Checkmates

Dogs herd sheep by pressuring them, nipping at their heels and doing whatever it takes to push them in one direction. And that's what *you're* doing in all the basic checkmates – "herding" the enemy King up against the edge of the board (onto rank 1, rank 8, file a or file h).

In two of the five basic checkmates you must force the King into one of the four corner squares (**a1**, **a8**, **h1** or **h8**).

How?

By slowly restricting the King's movement until he has nowhere else to go.

The problem is that no player wants to be checkmated. In the hands of a good player, the King can be as slippery as a wet bar of soap!

So when you're going for one of the basic checkmates you need to really work at it.

You have to do three things:

1. **Visualize it!**

   Picture in your mind what the final checkmate will look like. Visualize where your pieces and the enemy King are going to end up.

2. **Plan it!**

   Set up a strategy. Prepare which steps to take in order to make your mental picture a reality.

3. **Do it!**

   Once you've imagined and planned how to achieve the checkmate, the last step is to follow through and make it happen!

Now let's take a look at what to *visualize*, *plan* and *do* for each of the basic checkmates.

White will be the checkmating side in all of the examples, but the steps are exactly the same if you are playing as Black.

These checkmates will get harder as we go, so be patient and give yourself as much time as you need to learn them.

Basic Checkmate #1: Two Rooks vs. King

This is the easiest checkmate of them all and usually the first one that beginners understand.

Visualize it!

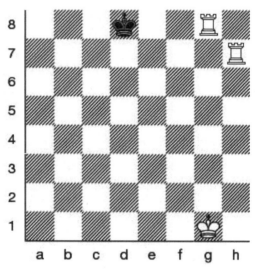

Figure 9-4

- The enemy King must be on a back rank.
- One of your Rooks must control the rank that the King is on and the other must control the next rank.
- There must be at least one empty square between the King and both of your Rooks (so that he can't capture either of them).
- Your own King can be anywhere, as long as he's out of the way. He will not be part of the attack.

Plan it!

1. Use your Rooks to take ranks away from the enemy King, forcing him to retreat.

2. Once one of your Rooks has the King pinned up against the edge of the board, bring your other Rook in for the checkmate.

Do it!

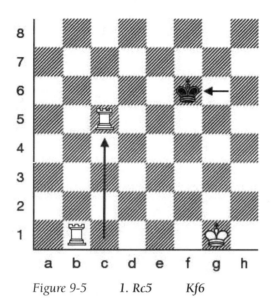

Figure 9-5   *1. Rc5*   *Kf6*

First, place one of your Rooks on the rank in front of the enemy King.

Since the Rook controls the entire rank, this instantly traps the King on that side of the board. He can only move backward or sideways.

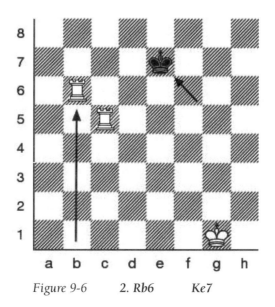

Figure 9-6   *2. Rb6*   *Ke7*

Now bring your second Rook onto the same rank as the enemy King. This will put him in check, and force him to retreat back toward the edge of the board.

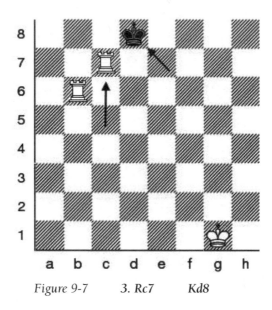

Figure 9-7   3. Rc7   Kd8

Go back to your first Rook and do the same thing. Put him on the same rank as the King.

(Check!) The King will have to take another step backward.

Watch out! It won't always happen, but if the enemy King gets too close to one of your Rooks (do you see the threat in *Figure 9-7*?) there's another step.

You'll have to use a couple of extra moves to get the Rooks out of his reach.

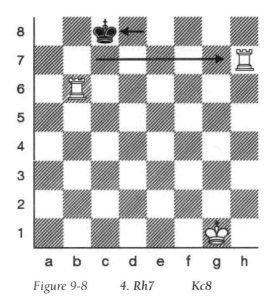

Figure 9-8   *4. Rh7*   *Kc8*

The Rook protects himself by moving all the way to the other side of the board.

Black then moves **Kc8** and is controlling square **b8**. If White moves **Rb8**, Black will capture the Rook!

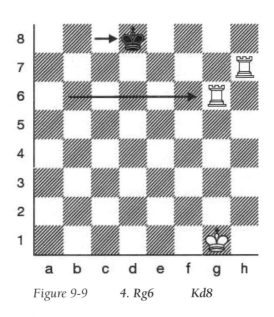

Figure 9-9   *4. Rg6*   *Kd8*

No problem; White just moves his other Rook to safety.

Black tries to head back toward the Rooks, but it's no use.

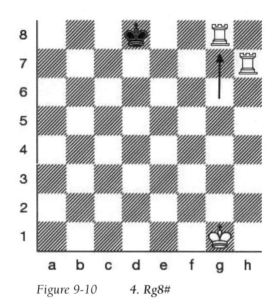

Figure 9-10   4. Rg8#

The **g** Rook comes in for the final blow.

That's it. A very simple checkmate!

A checkmate with the two Rooks is sometimes called "the lawn-mower" because of the way the Rooks cut down every blade of grass until the King has nowhere left to hide.

This one shouldn't give you much trouble, but here are a few things to look out for:

- Keep your Rooks close together but not right on top of each other. Don't blockade them; they need passing space.

- Always leave space between the Rooks and the enemy King – don't let him get close enough to take one of your Rooks! If the King moves toward your Rooks, move them to safety.

Basic Checkmate #2: Rook and King vs. King

It might take some time to understand this checkmate, but if you're careful and pay attention you'll be able to work it out.

In this checkmate, and in all the rest, your King will actually get involved in the attack. Up to now he hasn't been much of an attacking piece, but when almost all of your pieces are gone, the one or two left need all the help they can get!

Visualize it!

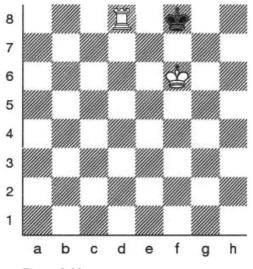

Figure 9-11

- The enemy King must be on a back rank or file.

- Your Rook controls the rank or file that the King is on, with at least one open square between them so that the King can't capture the Rook.

- The two Kings stand face to face, directly across from each other, with one open rank or file between them.

Plan it!

In some ways this checkmate is like the checkmate with the two Rooks.

It's the same idea: Push the enemy King up against the edge of the board and checkmate him there.

But now you're going to have to use your King to help push him. And since the King doesn't control as many squares as a Rook, it's harder to do.

Before we get into the plan, let's look at two diagrams. It's Black's turn to move in each of these positions.

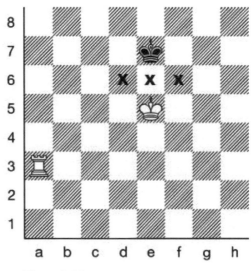

Figure 9-12

The White King is taking away all of the squares that Black's King could move to on the 6th rank.

When two Kings face each other this way (directly across from each other with one open rank or file between them), it's called *opposition*.

An important thing to remember about chess is that a King can *never* step into any of the eight squares around another King, since that would be stepping into check.

The way Kings restrict each other's movements is by using opposition.

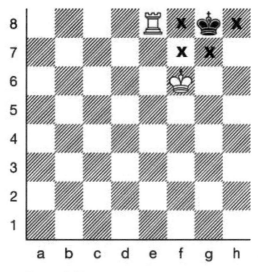

Figure 9-13

The Rook is checking Black's King, but it's not a checkmate because the Kings are not in opposition. But if White's King was just one square to the right, on **g6**, the Kings would be in opposition and it would be checkmate.

Keep in mind that unless you're in opposition, you can never cut off the other King's movement!

Now let's get to our plan for this checkmate:

1. Use your Rook, with your King standing guard next to him, to slowly cut off squares from the enemy King. *Box him in and push him back!*

2. Once the King has been pushed up against the side of the board, pin him there with your Rook and bring your King to the next rank.

3. Now the King is trapped on the edge. Move your King and Rook around to force the enemy King to step into opposition with your King.

4. Once the two Kings are in opposition, move your Rook up to the rank that the enemy King is standing on, making sure that there's at least one open square between your Rook and the enemy King so that he can't attack.

5. All of his squares are cut off. Checkmate!

Do it!

Start by setting up your board like this:

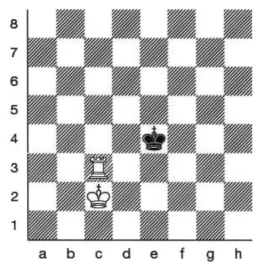

Figure 9-14

The Black King is in the center, so you have your work cut out for you. Remember, you have to push him up against the edge.

Follow along to see how we'll do that.

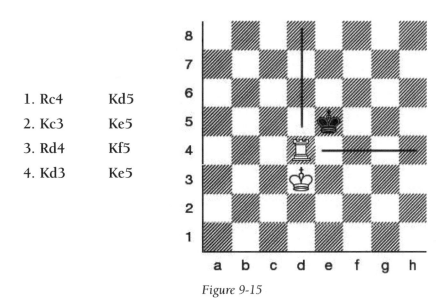

1. Rc4   Kd5

2. Kc3   Ke5

3. Rd4   Kf5

4. Kd3   Ke5

Figure 9-15

Now we're putting on the pressure, with the Rook and King backing each other up every step of the way.

Notice how we're gently pushing the Black King, moving him over to the side and up to the top. *Over and up, over and up.*

The lines show the box we are making around the Black King. He can never take our Rook as long as our King is standing nearby.

Guarding your Rook is the most important thing to do in this checkmate. If you let the Black King capture him, the game will have to end in a draw.

A King by himself can't checkmate another King!

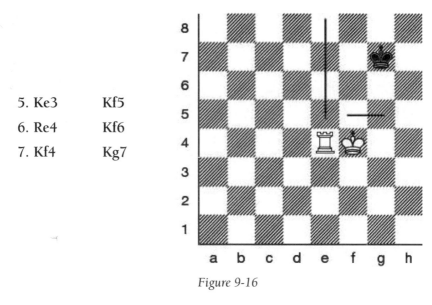

5. Ke3   Kf5

6. Re4   Kf6

7. Kf4   Kg7

Figure 9-16

The White King has moved up to the fourth rank.

Black is running scared and moving back.

Just keep pressing! *Over and up.*

The Black King's box is getting smaller and smaller. Even better, he's almost up against the edge.

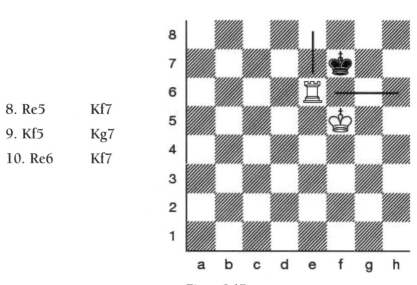

8. Re5   Kf7

9. Kf5   Kg7

10. Re6   Kf7

Figure 9-17

Good! Now the Black King is stuck in a very small box and all he can do is run around in it. White's next move will force him up against the top edge.

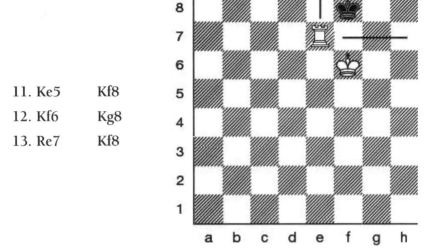

11. Ke5	Kf8
12. Kf6	Kg8
13. Re7	Kf8

Figure 9-18

The Black King is right where we want him; the Rook has him pinned against the back rank.

Now all you have to do is a little dancing to force the Black King to step into opposition with your King.

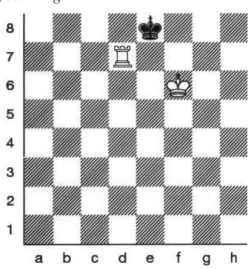

14. Ke6	Kg8
15. Rd7	Kf8
16. Kf6	Ke8

Figure 9-19

Here is the important moment.

Look at the position above carefully. What's happening?

First, the Black King is threatening your Rook. You could bring your King to e6 to protect him but that doesn't get you anywhere in getting the checkmate.

Now think about what squares your King is controlling: e7 and f7. The Black King can't move anywhere on rank 7 on his next move, except to take your Rook.

What next?

Everything is in place . . . Is there a move you can make that will force the King into opposition without ruining the position?

17. Rd1   Kf8

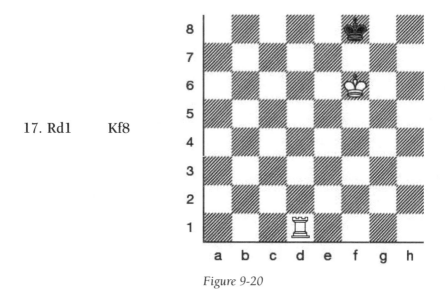

Figure 9-20

The solution is to play what's called a "waiting move."

Remember that no matter where the Rook is on file d, he controls the whole file, so just move him somewhere along file d! It makes no difference how far.

The point is that on the edge of the board a King's range of movement is only five squares.

Your King controls **e7** and **f7** and your Rook controls **d7** and **d8**. So that leaves only one legal move: **Kf8**.

And that move forces him to step into opposition with your King!

18. Rd8#

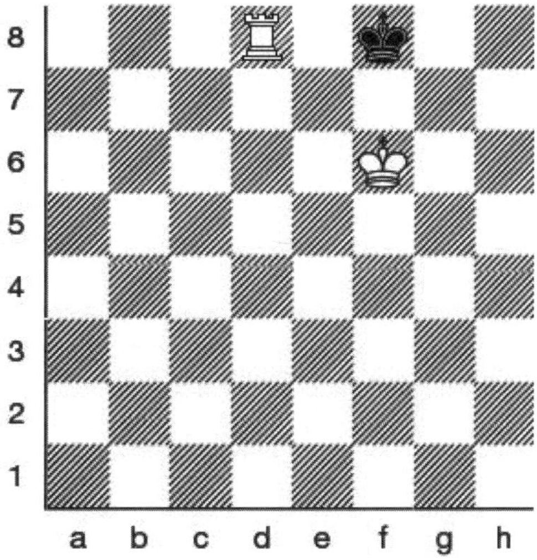

Figure 9-21

Now your Rook comes up to rank 8 to deliver the final checkmate. The game is over.

As you can see, this checkmate takes some careful movement, especially for the final step.

Getting the other King to step into opposition with yours isn't always easy, especially if the other player knows what you're trying to do.

Sometimes the enemy King will just hop back and forth on the same two squares. But if you think carefully and play a waiting move, you can chase him into the corner, and then he'll have nowhere to step but into opposition.

Here are some things to remember for this checkmate:

- Make sure that your King is protecting your Rook at all times. The enemy King will be waiting for you to make a mistake and leave the Rook open to capture. If that happens, the game will be a draw.

- Sometimes you might drive the King over to the edge, but it will be up and down along a file, instead of left to right along a rank. The steps to checkmating are the same; you'll just be doing it sideways.

- Be careful not to put your Rook on the same rank or file as the enemy King unless he is in opposition with your King. He will hop right out of the box you've been trying to build and you'll have to start all over again.

You might not understand this checkmate yet, but follow the book with a board and chess pieces a few times. Pay attention to what is happening and try to think about what each move means.

The next step, the real test, is to set up the Rook and two Kings in a different position, however you like, and to do the checkmate from scratch.

If you've paid attention, you'll know exactly what to do. Have a friend play the Black King or just play him yourself.

Basic Checkmate #3: Queen and King vs. King

This checkmate is very easy if you know what to do – or, perhaps, if you know what *not* to do!

But keep in mind that Queen and King vs. King is the most dangerous of all the basic checkmates.

How? I'll get to that. But first let's see what it looks like.

Visualize it!

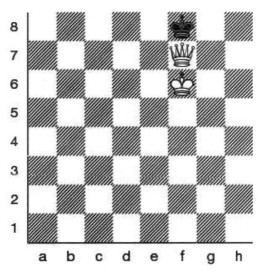

Figure 9-22

This checkmate can take many different forms, but in all of them the enemy King will be pressed against the edge of the board.

The Queen delivers check. Your King will either be guarding her or controlling the enemy King's escape squares.

Plan it!

It works just like the Rook and King checkmate: Your Queen makes a box around the enemy King, pressuring him to move back, while your King stands guard over her.

The danger to you comes when the enemy King is on the edge of the board.

Don't Fall into the Stalemate Trap

By now you know that the Queen is a very powerful piece. But when it comes to checkmating, she's almost too powerful for her own good!

I told you what a stalemate is in Chapter 2, but let's go over it again in more detail.

A stalemate is one of the ways in which a chess game can end in a draw. Neither player wins or loses.

It happens when . . .

1. It's a player's turn to move and the only piece she can move is her King.
2. Her King is not in check.
3. The only move she can make would put her King in check.
4. Since moving into check is an illegal move, the player can't make *any* move. The game ends in a draw.

Here's a simple idea that will help you remember the stalemate rule: *You can't spell "checkmate" without "check!"*

Your final move of the game must be a move that puts the King into check.

Here are some examples of stalemate:

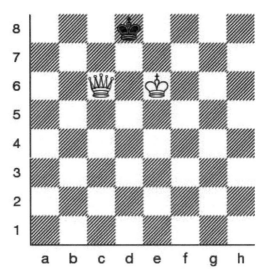

Figure 9-23

It's Black's turn to move. There are 5 open squares around his King.

White's Queen controls **c8**, **f8** and **c7**; White's King controls **e7**. They both control **d7**.

Black's King is *not* in check, but he has no legal move.

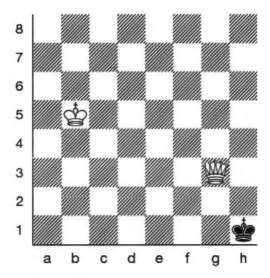

Figure 9-24

The Queen is so powerful that a stalemate can happen even when her King isn't nearby.

The three squares around the Black King – **g1**, **g2** and **h2** – are controlled by White's Queen.

But again, Black is *not* actually in check. It's his turn to move but he can't move anywhere.

Stalemate.

It Can Happen to You!

Don't think that a stalemate is rare; in fact, it's very common.

It's easier than you think for a careful opponent to set a stalemate trap – and you can bet that sometimes your opponent is going to try!

Other times, neither of you will see the stalemate coming. You'll fall into it by accident and only realize what has happened when it's too late.

Every beginner will probably fall into stalemate at least once.

The most important part of your plan for the Queen and King vs.

King checkmate is to avoid stalemate.

When the King gets close to the edge of the board, you need to be extra alert. Look for possible stalemates before making any move.

The rest of the plan for this checkmate is the same as it was for the Rook and King mate, except that sometimes you don't have to get the two Kings into opposition.

Do it!

Start here:

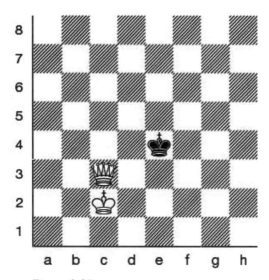

Figure 9-25

If you remember the Rook and King vs. King checkmate, this setup will be familiar.

You know what to do. Start pushing.

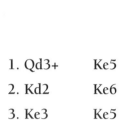

1. Qd3+   Ke5
2. Kd2   Ke6
3. Ke3   Ke5

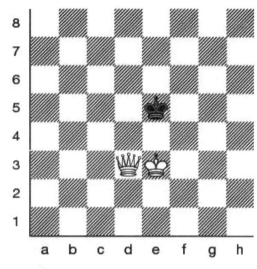

Figure 9-26

Notice that you checked the King on your first move. You will get more checks as you push him toward the edge simply because of how many squares the Queen controls.

It's much easier for the Queen to force the King up against the edge.

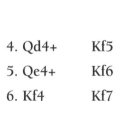

4. Qd4+   Kf5
5. Qe4+   Kf6
6. Kf4   Kf7

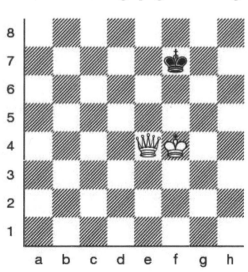

Figure 9-27

Good work! He's almost up against the edge already.

7. Qe5   Kf8

8. Kf5   Kf7

9. Qe6+   Kf8

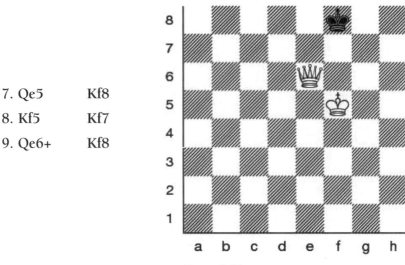

Figure 9-28

Now the Black King is up against the edge of the board.

He's not stuck yet, though. Bring your Queen up to trap him there.

Be very careful from now on. Watch every move and make sure to keep an eye out for stalemate possibilities.

10. Qd7   Kg8

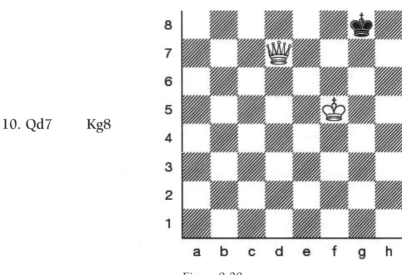

Figure 9-29

Now you've brought your Queen up to rank 7 and the King is trapped. Bring your own King up to rank 6 and you'll be ready to checkmate.

11. Kf6   Kf8

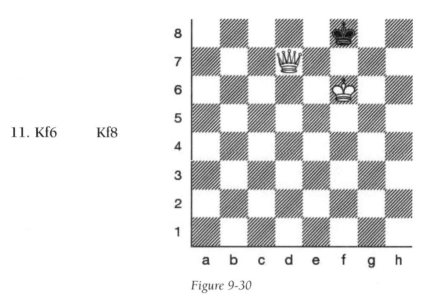

Figure 9-30

Your King steps up, and the enemy King steps right into opposition.

You actually have a choice of checkmate squares. You could checkmate him on **d8**, like the Rook would, or you can checkmate him on **f7**.

It's up to you.

12. Qf7#

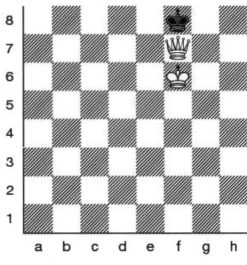

Figure 9-31

That's it!

If you can checkmate with Rook and King, you can checkmate with Queen and King; they play out almost exactly the same.

The only difference is that you have to be watch for a stalemate once the King is up against the board edge.

Basic Checkmate #4:
Bishops and King vs. King

This checkmate is harder than the first three – and it can also be the most frustrating! Pay close attention.

Visualize it!

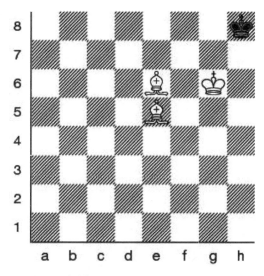

Figure 9-32

- The enemy King will always be in a corner square: **a1, a8, h1 or h8**.
- One Bishop gives check.
- The other Bishop covers an escape square.
- Your King covers the other two escape squares.

Plan it!

The problem with this checkmate is that pushing the enemy King is harder with Bishops.

Why?

Because they don't attack head-on, so the enemy King can find a lot of openings to jump through if you're not making just the right moves.

Getting your opponent's King to the edge is only the first step. Then you have to carefully push him into the corner while avoiding dangerous stalemate traps.

Here's the plan:

1. Bring your Bishops and King to the center of the board, keeping them together in tight formation.

2. Lead each of your pieces forward, one step at a time, to pressure the King up against the edge. Keep your formation!

3. Once the enemy King is on the edge, bring your Bishops up to force him toward the corner.

4. Get the two Kings in opposition, or close to it, to help pin the enemy King into place.

5. Bring your Bishops back down, step by step, until the King is stuck in the corner and checkmated.

Do it!

Start here:

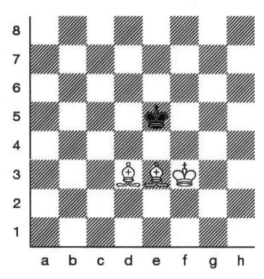

Figure 9-33

Just like in the other checkmates, you can't lose as long as your King is close and standing guard over the Bishops.

Protecting them is important. If either Bishop gets captured, the game will be a draw.

Unlike a Rook, you cannot force checkmate with just one Bishop and your King.

Let's get moving.

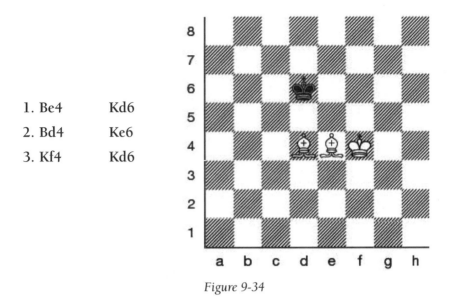

1. Be4   Kd6
2. Bd4   Ke6
3. Kf4   Kd6

Figure 9-34

If you look at the lines on the diagram, you'll be able to visualize what is happening.

What we're doing this time is using the Bishops to make a big triangle around the King.

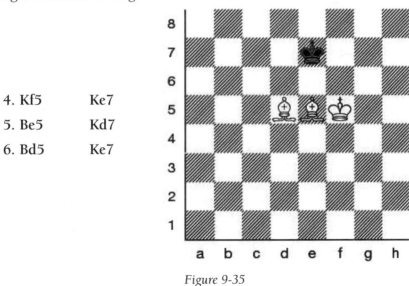

4. Kf5   Ke7
5. Be5   Kd7
6. Bd5   Ke7

Figure 9-35

Notice how this diagram looks like the last one, and the last one looks like the one before it. It's the same triangle, just getting smaller.

Your Bishops and King are on the same files; the only difference is that they're slowly moving up the ranks.

The Bishops come up by stepping forward and around each other in a criss-cross motion and the King leads the way when he needs to.

Criss-cross, King

King, criss-cross

7. Be6   Kd8

8. Kf6   Ke8

9. Bc7   Kf8

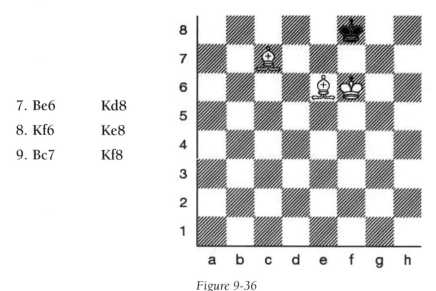

Figure 9-36

Now the Bishops come up to rank 7 to threaten rank 8 squares and push the King toward the corner.

Your King does his part by taking away options on rank 7.

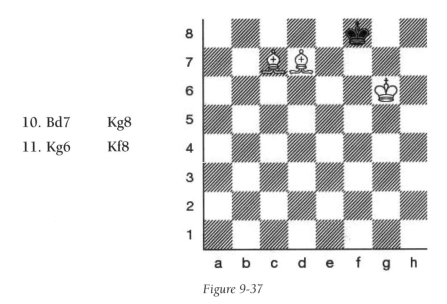

10. Bd7   Kg8
11. Kg6   Kf8

Figure 9-37

Your opponent's King is now trying to get away to the only unguarded square, **Ke7** – but you can hold him in place.

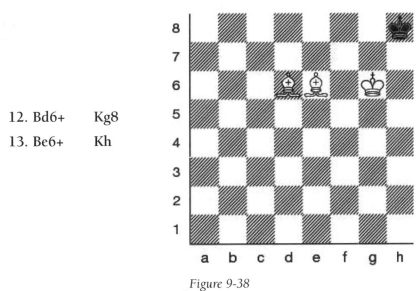

12. Bd6+   Kg8
13. Be6+   Kh

Figure 9-38

The dark square Bishop steps down to check the King on **d6**, which forces him to move to **g8**.

Then the light square Bishop comes down to check him again on **e6**!

The King is stuck right in the corner where we want him: on **h8**.

Time to finish him off.

14. Be5#

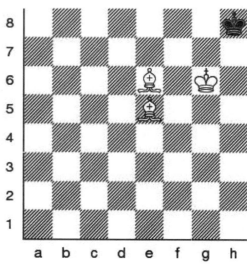

Figure 9-39

The dark square Bishop steps down once more. The King is checkmated!

If this checkmate seems a bit complicated, try to think of the steps as a rhythm:

Criss-cross, King

Criss-cross, King

King, criss-cross

Bishop up, Bishop up, King

Bishop down, Bishop down, Bishop down

There are other ways of getting this checkmate too, and the pieces can end up in many different formations. But the way I've showed you is the easiest and it works just as well.

Now do this one yourself. Try using the same steps to checkmate the King in all four corners of the board.

You'll make mistakes at first and will probably get a few stalemates, but be patient. You'll eventually get a feel for how the checkmate actually works.

The key is that the Bishops don't directly attack the King. If you look at the example again you'll notice that what the Bishops are really attacking is the space *around* the King.

Practicing this checkmate will help you understand one of the main ideas in winning chess: Empty squares are never just empty squares – they're space.

And learning how to control that space is as important as learning how to control the chess pieces.

Basic Checkmate #5:
One Bishop, One Knight and the King

This is by far the most difficult of the basic checkmates. It takes a lot of patience and skill.

Visualize it!

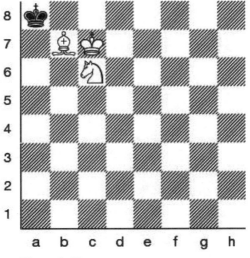

Figure 9-40

- The enemy King will always be in a corner square – **a1**, **a8**, **h1** or **h8**.
- If you have a dark square Bishop, the King will be checkmated on a dark square; if you have a light square Bishop, he will be checkmated on a light square.

Plan it!

1. Force the King to the edge.
2. Force the King to the dark or light corner (depending on which Bishop you are using).

Do it!

You're on your own for this one. There is no easy step-by-step formula for this checkmate.

In fact, the truth is that it's a little too tough for a beginner. You may want to skip this one for now and come back to it when you have more playing experience.

But I'm not saying that you shouldn't attempt to figure out this checkmate. Practicing it will do wonders for your visualization skills, and will go a long way in showing you the strengths and weaknesses of the Bishop and Knight.

If you work it out, congratulations. It's no easy task.

Other Checkmates

There are hundreds of positions and possibilities when it comes to checkmates.

Learning how to visualize, plan and carry them out is a skill that every chess player needs.

Checkmating isn't easy! Don't expect to pick it up right away.

But don't worry. As you play more games, you'll learn to see them coming all the way from middle game.

Before we finish our discussion of checkmates, there are three important ones that you should know about.

Smothered Mate

A "smothered mate" is when the King is in check and can't move because he's surrounded by his own chess pieces.

Take a look at this smothered mate game that was played in Poland in 1950:

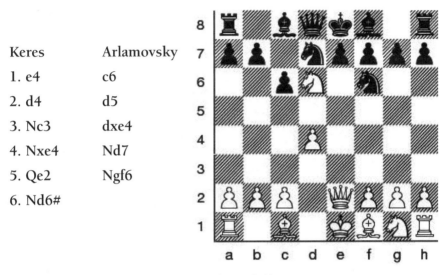

Keres	Arlamovsky
1. e4	c6
2. d4	d5
3. Nc3	dxe4
4. Nxe4	Nd7
5. Qe2	Ngf6
6. Nd6#	

Figure 9-41

White's Knight checks the King, but Black's e7 pawn can't capture the Knight.

Do you see why?

Always keep your eyes peeled for a possible smothered mate when your King is surrounded by his own forces. Leave him some room to move.

It's true that leaving the King unprotected is a mistake, but sometimes he can be *too* protected!

Fool's Mate

I told you earlier that it's best to move out a center pawn first in the opening. This checkmate is one of the reasons why.

Watch what can happen if you move your **f** pawn like this:

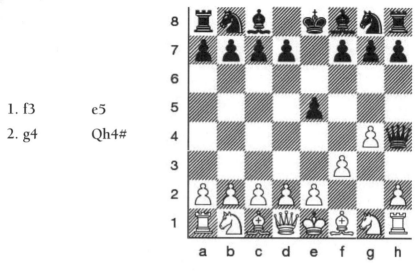

1. f3   e5
2. g4   Qh4#

Figure 9-42

White's **f** pawn moved out and left his King wide open for an attack. It was very simple for Black to jump at the opportunity and checkmate him almost instantly.

"Fool's mate" shows how important it is to keep the King safe.

Fool's mate is the fastest chess game you'll ever see – and it's also pretty embarrassing if you're the fool who falls for it.

Scholar's Mate

Here's a checkmate that you *must* know about, because it's a simple trap that many players will try to set up.

Pay attention, especially if you ever plan to compete in a tournament.

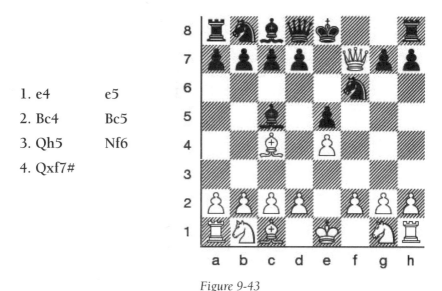

1. e4   e5
2. Bc4   Bc5
3. Qh5   Nf6
4. Qxf7#

Figure 9-43

The White Queen gives check and the White Bishop backs her up. Checkmate!

You can see how easy it is to fall into this checkmate.

Black chose two smart first moves but got checkmated anyway.

How could he have prevented this?

The answer is to move **Qe7** just after White moves **Qh5**. Now the Black Queen protects the **f7** square.

Problem solved.

But even better, White's Queen is stuck out in the open! Black can take advantage of this by using his pieces to harass her.

Putting the Queen in danger is the risk of scholar's mate. If the other player sees it coming and defends it, your Queen is a sitting duck.

This is why I recommend that you don't try it yourself.

But many people also see scholar's mate as a dirty trick, played by a person who doesn't want an honest game of chess. So it might be a good idea to leave it alone.

Beware of scholar's mate from another player, but don't play it yourself. You can do better.

Know Your Checkmates

Hopefully your head isn't spinning after reading about all of these checkmates.

I didn't intend to overwhelm you; I've just discussed them so much because they're at the heart of good chess.

Nothing will help you learn this game more deeply than studying endgames and checkmates.

Practice them and you'll be on your way to winning!

Chapter 10

Be a Champion!

Congratulations! You've made it. You now have a good handle on the basics of winning chess.

You've managed to take your understanding of the game to a whole new level – and good for you!

There are a large number of players who only know how the chess pieces move and the basic rules of the game. But when it comes down to the deeper, more challenging ideas, they don't know a Knight fork from a salad fork!

But you . . . Well, you can read chess game notation.

You have a sense of what to do in the opening.

You recognize what to do in difficult middle game situations.

You can force checkmates in the endgame.

Maybe you're even getting an idea of how to come up with plans and strategies.

These are all impressive abilities that you can – and should – be proud of.

Get Out There and Play

The most important thing for you to understand after reading this book is that you've only taken your first step in a journey that lasts a lifetime.

The next step is for you to play real chess games against real opponents – your little brother, your friends, your chess club or even your computer.

As a beginner you'll make lots of mistakes. You'll get frustrated; you'll get checkmated.

You'll lose – and you'll lose often.

And you may even wonder why you ever bothered reading this book.

But remember that all you have right now is education. What you *don't* have, and what you need, is experience!

The simplest way to put it is this: Education + Experience = Learning.

You haven't *learned* chess yet – and you won't until you've played many games.

Reading this book doesn't guarantee that you'll win. It is only meant to steer you in the right direction, to prepare you with a bit of education.

It's up to you to add the experience.

Staying on the Path

If you keep at it through the rough beginning, after a while you *will* start winning.

When you have many chess games under your belt you'll start to recognize patterns in certain situations.

As you learn, your ability to deal with them will become stronger. You'll become more confident about what to do with each and every move.

But as you gather experience, don't let your education slide.

This book only scratches the surface of what there is to be said about chess. There are hundreds of additional books that focus in-depth on specific aspects of the game.

There are books on openings, on tactics, on tournament play – anything and everything you can imagine.

The bottom line is this: When your *experience* moves past the beginner phase, so should your *education*!

Always challenge yourself with new ideas. Push your game in new directions.

As you discover weaknesses in your game (and you will), seek out books to help you.

If your middle game play isn't strong, check out books that concentrate on this stage. If you have trouble finding checkmates, many books are written specifically to enhance your ability to see checkmate opportunities.

You can even get a little adventurous with your studies.

Did you know that some chess players can play the game blindfolded? It's true! There are books that will teach you all about this technique.

When it comes to chess, you are never "finished." A player who thinks he has nothing left to learn really has a *whole lot* to learn!

Mastering the Basics

Have you ever left home on a long trip and when you returned everything seemed different to you?

Maybe things that you ignored before suddenly jumped out at you, or you simply saw your surroundings in a new light.

This happens during the process of learning – in chess, and in everything else. Things sometimes seem different after a period of time or after you've learned more about them.

During your life as a chess player, always take the time to "come back home" and get a fresh look at the basics.

Many teachers and books rush past the simple steps to concentrate on the more sophisticated and advanced theories. They lose sight of how much can be learned by just working and re-working the basics.

For those new to the game, the basics introduce you to the skills and knowledge that you need to develop. But when experienced players come back to the basics, they find a lot that they missed or did not appreciate when they learned them the first time around.

You can't know that you missed something important until experience shows you that you missed it! In fact, you need experience to truly understand the basics at all.

If there's a problem in your game, the trick is often just to come back and start over again from a new perspective. The answer could be right there!

But you need experience to recognize it.

Attitude is Everything

The purpose of this book isn't just to show you how pawns are moved or how the Rook and King can force a checkmate. These are only instructions on how to play chess.

This book is also about learning important life lessons.

Chess is a duel – a duel with your opponent *and* a duel with yourself. It will test your integrity, your intelligence, your nerve and your determination to succeed.

It will also test your willingness to learn and to think.

When you're setting up at the beginning of the game, it's just as important to position your chess pieces as it is to position your mind!

With each move around the board, you must make moves in your mind – and not just in terms of strategy and tactics, but in thought and feeling as well.

If your goal is only to play a game and win at it, you're wasting your time; winning isn't the point.

You should play to learn, whether you're winning or losing, from opponents who will show you new things.

If you approach chess in this way, it will pay off. You'll be able to apply the lessons of the game to your daily life.

The key to enjoying, and getting the most out of, chess (or any game, for that matter) is having the right attitude.

Pass it On

Each of us has the power to touch the lives of others in a positive way.

If you take the time to stop and think, there are probably many people who have encouraged and supported you to become who you are.

It might be members of your family: parents, siblings, grandparents, aunts and uncles. It could be teachers who believed in you, friends who trusted you or even strangers who simply graced your darker days with a smile.

The important thing to realize is that whatever their act, big or small, they each made a difference in your life in some way.

An important part of living a happy, successful life is to learn that when you are given something you should try to give something in return. And when it comes to knowledge, the easiest way is to simply pass on what you've learned.

If you decide to pursue chess, find at least one person you care about and pass it on. Teach them the rules, strategies and ideas I've shared with you in this book.

Choose to make a difference in someone else's life. Whether or not they use the knowledge is up to them, but either way you've given them something they can benefit from.

Think of this: Very few people ever regretted taking up chess!

The Last Word

On August 28, 1963, on the steps of the Lincoln Memorial in Washington, D.C., Dr. Martin Luther King, Jr. began his famous speech with these words:

"I have a dream."

What followed was a vision that forever changed our nation.

Yet many people today regard their visions and dreams as if they are impossible fantasies. They don't believe that their dreams will come true unless a miracle happens.

Start every chess game thinking of Dr. King's words. Dream that you can win.

If you lose, that's okay. But keep the dream alive, and dream it again the next time you play.

It worked for me.

In 1999, I entered the Birmingham citywide chess championship with the dream of winning. I prepared myself by reading every book I could get my hands on, talking to great players and studying what they did to succeed.

Although others thought I was the least likely to win, I was determined to see myself as a champion.

I was determined to dream.

Not only did my dream come true that year, but also the next. I became the first African-American to win back-to-back citywide chess tournaments in my hometown of Birmingham, Alabama.

And I achieved this honor because of my determination, my persistence and my willingness to believe in a dream.

I've failed many times in my life – and believe me, it doesn't feel good. But I've also learned to take away something from each of my failures in order to move on to the next level of success.

Play chess. You may fail; you may succeed.

But you will improve, learn and dream . . . one move at a time.

A Winner's Creed

If you think you are beaten, you are.

If you think you dare not, you don't.

If you'd like to win, but think you can't,
It's almost a cinch you won't.

If you think you'll lose, you're lost.

All over the world we find that
Success begins with a person's faith;
It's all a state of mind.

Life's battles don't always go to
the stronger or faster hand;
they go to the one who trusts the self...

And who always thinks, "I can."

—Anonymous

PART II

How to Play
and Win at Life:
Life Lessons
from Chess

Life Lesson 1
Follow the Masters

One of the secrets to becoming a successful chess player is to follow the masters. Literally.

Study exactly what moves chess masters make by looking over the written versions of their matches.

What you learn from the true masters will help you improve your own game.

But don't limit yourself to studying the masters of chess. Whatever you want to do in life, whether it be a sport like basketball, a talent like singing, or a trade like computer repair, follow the masters of those skills.

If you want to be as capable as they are, you can!

You can learn by example or you can learn by doing. The most successful people learn both ways.

So watch how the people you choose as masters act and listen to what they say. Then take action and do what they do.

Success leaves clues, so look for the clues the masters leave behind.

And if there's someone really famous you want to learn from, even if you don't get to meet them, you can still learn from them.

Go to your library or bookstore and see if there's a book by them or about them. Or look for their biography on TV, on A & E or E!

I promise you'll find something interesting that will shorten your path to success.

Don't be afraid you'll lose sight of who you are by copying someone else. It's not going to happen.

When you were born, you knew nothing. You had to learn everything you know from other people.

It's the choices you made about what you wanted to learn that make you the unique person you are now.

And even when you're following someone else's lead, you're going to apply what you've learned in your own personal way.

One thing that will help you along is to have at least one teacher, or coach who works with you toward attaining whatever knowledge or skill you want to have.

Teachers are treasures!

As you play chess, you'll begin to understand the need to find and follow a master. That's because you're going to lose a lot of games!

And there's nothing wrong with that.

In fact, that may be why you picked up this book in the first place.

So let me be your first chess coach, and allow me to help you become a skilled player. Gain from my experience by observing and following the advice in this book.

If you pay attention and follow through, you will be successful.

Life Lesson 2
Birds of a Feather

There's an old saying that goes "Birds of a feather flock together."

This saying means that similar people are naturally pulled toward each other. And it also means that you become like the people you spend time with.

If you hang out with crooks, there's a good chance you'll become a crook yourself. If you hang out with people who are negative and depressing, you'll become negative and depressing too.

Don't let this happen!

Take charge of the choices you make when it comes to the people you spend your time with.

It's one of life's easiest formulas: positive desire brings positive people together and leads to positive results.

If you want to get better grades, spend time with other people who do well in school.

If you want to be more outgoing, spend time with outgoing people.

What you create for yourself, and for them, is a place of support and encouragement where everybody helps each other reach their goals.

I like to put it this way: Spend heavyweight time with heavyweight people, and lightweight time with lightweight people.

Your heavyweight people are the ones who share your dreams and desires, and who want to see you attain them.

Your lightweight people are the ones who don't help you, or who stand in the way and block your path.

You might be wondering what this has to do with chess.

Everything!

Chess is played by those seeking positive rewards. They want to expand their minds, to learn about themselves, and just to experience the fun and thrills that the game offers.

If you're reading this book, you obviously have at least some desire for those things too.

If you want to improve at chess, the only way to do it is to seek out others who play.

They shouldn't be too hard to find. In fact, they're all around you.

These are the birds you're looking for. Get together with them and soar.

♚Life Lesson 3
Work Within the Rules

One of the reasons that human beings are able to live in societies together is because most people choose to follow a set of rules and laws.

Rules create order, and order creates a safe environment for people to live, succeed and be happy.

Nobody wants to follow all the rules, all the time. Sometimes we just want to do what feels good, or what will benefit us, or to avoid an unpleasant responsibility. But if everyone acted this way all the time, we would all lose out in the long run.

We trade our desire to act selfishly for the benefits that come from cooperating with others.

For that cooperation to exist, there needs to be a common set of expectations that everyone follows.

Chess is the same way. It has rules so that neither player has an advantage over the other, and so that the game has a structure and a purpose.

Without a set of strictly defined rules, there would be no game at all!

You'd have a board and chesspieces, with no clear way to determine how to play or how to win.

There will be times when you want your pawn to hop four squares, or when you'll wish that your Rook could move diagonally and take out the Knight that's threatening your King.

But you've got to play the game the way it's meant to be played. Otherwise, winning has no value and losing has no meaning.

Working within a set of rules makes you smarter and more creative. It forces you to find answers and solutions when things don't line up your way.

Life is really a series of games, all with their own rules and skill requirements.

If you are going to win the game of life, you have to understand the rules. You have to know the penalties associated with breaking those rules, and the rewards for following them.

Every time you make a choice between following a rule, or ignoring it to do what you want, you are really making a choice between order and disorder.

Try to look at rules and limitations as a test, one that will make you stronger and better if you pass.

Games only work because they have rules.

Life is the same way.

When you're following the rules you're doing the right thing for everyone.

♔Life Lesson 4
Perfect Practice

I don't believe that the old saying "practice makes perfect" says enough. In my experience, real perfection takes more than just practice! It takes practicing in an effective, correct fashion.

In other words, practice does not make perfect. *Perfect practice* makes perfect.

The quality of the time you spend practicing is more important than the amount of time you spend practicing.

Even though you need to put in the hours, they have to be hours well spent.

If you sit down at your piano, or at your drawing table, or your chess board, you can't just go through the same simple routine you've done a hundred times before and expect to improve.

You need to remind yourself that the purpose of practicing is to discover what you're doing right, and what you're doing wrong.

Practice should be as much a process of thought as a process of actions.

Question yourself. Look at every move you make and determine whether or not it's a good move or a bad one.

When you practice chess, or anything else you want to improve at, it's really about developing the right habits and eliminating the wrong ones.

When your moves are correct, repeat them until they become automatic responses you don't even have to think about.

When your moves are incorrect, see them for what they are: Try to understand why you're making mistakes and do your best not to make them again.

Habits don't form by themselves, but you can help keep them from forming.

Get to know as many of your own personal habits as you can.

Build on the good ones and tear down the bad ones. Then you will be able to practice perfectly.

Life Lesson 5
Watch the Moves Other People Make

In chess, one way to guarantee that you'll lose is to ignore what your opponent is doing.

If you tune everything else out and only think about your OWN moves, you're missing half the game!

Sure, you can always look to see where the enemy chesspieces are, but you need to go deeper than that.

Watch your opponent's moves as they happen and try to get into their heads.

"What is she up to?" "Why did he do that?" "Is this a trap?"

They're not going to tell you straight out what they're planning, so you have to watch, listen, and figure it out for yourself.

Inspect what you expect!

People are the same way when they leave the chessboard.

They keep their intentions hidden, they say and do things that aren't what they seem on the surface, and they set all sort of tricks and traps.

The unfortunate fact of life is that not everybody's going to be on your side all the time. So pay attention to the moves they make and prepare yourself.

You can't control the wind, but you can set the sails.

Even when someone isn't competing with or opposing you, they're going to have their own reasons for keeping things to themselves.

If someone has hurt feelings, or is afraid, or lonely, they might not always speak out.

But if you're "watching their moves" you might pick up on these things and be able to help.

It is a kind of generosity; It makes you a more valued companion and strengthens your bonds.

Playing chess leads you to understand and respect the way other people think. You learn to see what's going on behind their eyes.

You have to in order to win!

Take that away from your game and into your life. You'll be able to protect yourself from people who aren't looking out for you, and be a better friend to the people you care about.

♚Life Lesson 6
Respect Your Opponents

Chess always takes two. Without opponents, you wouldn't be able to play at all!

Everyone you play chess with gives you a gift.

They're not just putting aside their time and energy to play—by sitting down at the table they're showing that they consider you a worthy opponent.

They also give you the opportunity to learn something, maybe many things, and improve yourself over the course of the game.

Competition is everywhere, all the time, especially in today's world. For jobs, for resources, in classrooms, in sports arenas, in more forms, times and places than you can imagine.

You're going to be competing for something or other for your whole life. And one of the best skills you can develop is a healthy respect for all of your opponents.

Without challenges, we don't grow.

When other people compete with us, what they're really doing is pushing us to become stronger and better, while at the same time allowing us to see our own strengths and weaknesses.

We come to know ourselves through challenge and competition.

For that, our opponents deserve our appreciation.

The ability to recognize this is at the heart of sportsmanship.

Even if you go up against a rude or unpleasant opponent, he or she is still doing you a service, whether they know it or not.

So ignore them when they brag or insult you. You're going to benefit from the experience of winning or losing to them; if they choose to treat you badly, that's their problem.

Chess may be the purest, most civilized, and rewarding form of competition there is.

When you play, you and your opponent are locked in a match of creativity and mental strength.

In winning, you can become their teacher.

In losing, you learn to be humble.

Opponents are not your enemy, in chess, in sports, or wherever they may come from.

They do you the honor of holding up mirrors for you to see yourself, and open doorways to improvement.

Always respect them for that.

♔Life Lesson 7
Visualize

Before you make any move in chess you have to see it in your mind—you visualize it first.

What will this do for me? What might my opponent do in response? What will the board look like when I'm finished?

You also have to visualize in a larger sense during the game.

If you come up with a plan that's going to take several moves to accomplish, you have to see it all, one step at a time, before you make a move.

Everything starts in your mind.

If you imagine yourself doing something well, you are more likely to actually achieve that level of skill.

Visualization is a technique that is used by successful people in all fields because they know how powerful it is.

If you want to be a master at playing a sport, or an instrument, or chess, take a few minutes every day to sit quietly and imagine yourself playing with perfection.

Take anywhere from a few minutes to an hour, make yourself comfortable, and visualize.

See, hear, taste, smell and feel how you want to be. Imagine it as vividly and with as much detail as you can.

The stronger your thoughts are, the more likely they are to become real. This is not just daydreaming. It's as important as practice.

You will be amazed at your results.

I don't know of a better way to improve at visualization than by playing chess.

It's a game that forces you to see things before they happen and to make both long-term and short-term plans.

And when those plans work out, it increases your confidence at visualizing.

When you have to change your plan from what you pictured, or even when it doesn't work out at all, you have an opportunity to stop, look, and learn why your plan failed.

Either way, you become better prepared for your next task, at the chessboard or in life.

♚Life Lesson 8

Know Your Strengths and Weaknesses

One of our purposes in life is to discover where we have skill and where we lack it.

Sometimes we have to work hard and only become good at something after years of experience.

Other times we are shocked to discover a hidden talent we never knew we had.

Without a doubt, though, every person will naturally be pulled towards certain activities and away from others.

It's hard to develop as a person without a sense of which is which.

Without knowing our strengths, how can we seize their potential and make the most of them?

Without knowing our weaknesses, how can we practice and improve upon them?

Having that knowledge is one of the keys to success and happiness.

Chess is wonderful exercise for discovering yourself in that way. Playing it calls on so many different kinds of skills, and strongly reflects your personality.

If you watch yourself closely, a single game can tell you a lot and answer many questions: Am I the sort of person to take risks or am

I cautious? Do I plan well, or do I rush into things unprepared? Am I good at noticing opportunities and taking them? Can I think my way out of difficult problems? Can I get my chesspieces to work as a team, or do I focus too much on individuals? Do I lose my temper when things don't go my way, or am I gracious and patient in defeat?

Play enough games and you'll be able to answer these questions and others.

That's the first step.

The next is to try and improve in the areas that need work.

Don't beat yourself up just because you're not good at every aspect of the game, even MOST of them.

If you lose 50 games in a row but you make some brilliant moves in each one, you obviously have something to work with.

It's just a matter of figuring out what you do well and what you do poorly.

Finding your place in the world, deciding what you want to do with your life, is going to depend on how clearly you see yourself. And an accurate picture comes through knowledge of your strengths and weaknesses.

Playing chess will help you learn to test them.

♔Life Lesson 9
Go the Extra Mile

Playing chess, and playing it well, calls upon you to be self-demanding over and over again.

Learning how to play the game is easy, but pushing yourself to actually becoming skilled is something more. It takes time and discipline and a lot of hard work.

And even if you get to the point of beating every world champion alive, there's always going to be a higher level to aim for.

Losing games will make you hungry for rematches; a chance to try again and come out the winner this time.

And there's nothing like the feeling of failing, going back to learn more, then making a successful comeback.

It's addictive! You'll learn to stay hungry no matter what you're doing.

Former NBA superstar Julius "Dr. J" Irving once remarked "I demand more of myself than anyone else can ever expect."

There is a common thread among people who live by a similar ideal: they tend to be the most successful individuals in their fields.

You can only go as far in this world as you demand yourself to go.

Even winning shouldn't be enough. Be stronger than you believe you can be. Do a little more than you did the last time.

There will always be parents or teachers or bosses around who will push you to do your best. But they'll never be able to push you as hard as you can push yourself.

What they think is your best may be far less than your real potential.

Only you can discover that. So if the coach tells you to run 5 laps, see if you can run 6 or 7. Live this way and you will be rewarded again and again.

One thing is certain when you go the extra mile: there are never any traffic jams or speeding tickets!

Life Lesson 10
Always Look For a Better Move

Emmanuel Lasker, a former World Champion used to say "If you see a good move, don't make it. There's always a better move to make."

In chess and in life we must make hundreds of decisions every day. "What should I eat for breakfast?", "I'm going to watch TV and do my homework later", "Should I capture that Bishop with my Rook?"

The problem is that we often act before we've even thought about our options. Sometimes we don't even realize that we HAVE options!

You create your life through an unending series of choices. Some things are beyond your control, but the best way to take charge of your life is to accept the fact that you ARE the one in charge!

Realizing that is the first step. The next is to make the best choices that you can.

Always give yourself the time and the patience to look for more than one option.

A chess game can unfold in tens of thousands of different ways.

In the first move, your choices are limited. But 10 moves deep, there are hundreds of possibilities!

When you begin to see that the easiest or most obvious moves aren't always the best ones, you'll have taken a huge step in your development as a player.

Sure, you could take his Bishop with your Rook, and it would be a good move.

But wait. Stop and look at it all from a different angle. That's not the only play to make.

You could also set a trap for him. Come up with a more complicated scheme that will eventually win you much more than just his Rook.

Once you start looking more deeply into your chess options and you'll benefit from those extra few moments of thought.

Start looking more deeply into your life options, too. Creative decision-making will take you to places you never dreamed. Develop that creativity by always looking for as many options as you can.

♔Life Lesson 11

Every Action Has a Consequence

In chess, every move you make influences another move - the one your opponent will make in response.

His move will then influence YOUR next move, your next will influence his, and so on.

The effects of any and every move you make are going to echo, in some way or another, all the way to the end of the game.

A single move is a lot more than it may seem.

Sometimes the effects are big, sometimes small, sometimes good, and sometimes bad. Sometimes you feel them right away, sometimes you don't feel them until 20 moves have gone by.

But one way or another, your actions are going to come back and have an effect on you.

Thinking about a chess game this way can be a little scary.

It makes your responsibility seem huge every time it's your turn, even if you do something as simple as starting the game by pushing your pawn forward to e4.

But there's no getting away from it - that move will affect the entire game. You make it knowing that it gives you a better chance than other moves you might choose.

What if you had moved your f pawn up two squares instead?

This is a poor choice. You're probably going to feel the effects quickly, and they're not going to be good.

Positive actions, good moves, will eventually lead to positive outcomes. Negative actions or bad moves, will eventually lead to negative outcomes.

Either way there will always be some effect.

What you will notice as you play chess and review your games is that you can often point to one key move that changed everything.

It didn't seem like much at the time, but it ended up making all the difference.

Start looking at your life choices the same way. Every action you take, or fail to take, is going to affect you.

Choose your actions carefully, and do your best to make sure that your choices are positive ones. Sooner or later, you will feel the effects.

♚Life Lesson 12
The Right Move at the Right Time

Life often gives us wonderful opportunities, but we don't take advantage of them until it's too late.

Other times we get ourselves into trouble by doing or saying something when we shouldn't; when waiting or not acting would be a much better choice.

Knowing what moves to make isn't enough. You have to know when to make them.

The more you play chess, the more you understand how important this is.

A player who makes big moves too early or too late will lose control of the game.

A better player will let each specific situation guide her. There will be times when capturing your opponent's Knight is a great move, but it would have been a terrible mistake just one move ago!

It's the same move, just made at a different time and under different circumstances.

If your timing is off, everything can fall apart.

Don't get discouraged if you feel like your moves are smart, but they end up costing you material (or even the whole game).

You may have been on to something, but timing is always part of the bigger picture.

Sometimes it's not that your moves that are bad, but the point at which you choose to make them.

Once you recognize this in your chess games, you will recognize it in your life.

Deciding what to do is only half the process.

Deciding when is the rest.

Life Lesson 13
Think Strategically

The most successful people in the world all have something very simple in common: they plan. They would not be successful if they didn't.

It's never enough just to want something. You have to move yourself toward your goals a step at a time.

Your plan is your path. Without it you have nothing to stand on. If you have nothing to stand on, how can you expect to get where you want to be?

"Strategy" is how you plan in a chess game. Your goal is to win, and it'll be a lot harder to win if you have no strategy.

It doesn't need to be perfect. It doesn't need to be complete. And you can change it as the game goes on.

But you should always try to come up with some direction to follow during the game.

Otherwise you're going to wander aimlessly, hoping that things will work themselves out.

If you find yourself losing a lot of games, maybe this is your problem.

If you continue to do what you've always done, you're going to get what you've always got.

Break out of your routine and think. See if you can come up with a new way to play.

Take charge by making a plan!

Let's say that you're playing against an opponent who you know has a bad habit of leaving his King unprotected.

This is where planning comes in.

Focus your strategy around his weakness. Take advantage of it by moving your pieces around in a way that will be good for you, and bad for him.

Or you can base your strategy around your own strengths. For example, you know that you play better when there are less pieces on the board.

So your strategy for the game should be to try to exchange as many pieces as possible, as soon as possible.

The bottom line is that a strategy, a plan, gives you control. Control leads to confidence. And confidence leads to success.

As long as you build your strategy around your own abilities, or around the weaknesses of whatever it is you're up against, you will be shaping the outcome in your favor.

Life Lesson 14
Learn From Losing

Losing never feels good.

But what many people don't understand is that it doesn't have to be a *bad* feeling either.

The effect that losing has on you depends on your attitude.

Attitude is the scale you use to weigh the events that you experience. If your scale is out of balance, all of your measurements will be off!

Approach every chess game as a lesson first, and a contest second. You're trying to win of course, but more importantly you're trying to learn.

Start looking at it this way and I guarantee that you will play better, and happier. There's no way you're going to win every time, and it doesn't make sense to expect to.

As long as you can walk away from the game having learned or discovered something new, even if it seems small and unimportant, then playing was worthwhile.

It doesn't matter whether you won or lost.

I tell my students that anybody who loses a thousand chess games will be a master. That might sound strange, but it's true.

You will learn a lot more from losing than you will from winning, as long as you examine your games and look for why and how it happened.

If you do that, then you will become more knowledgeable with every loss.

Approach your whole life this way. Your failures and losses are really just opportunities in disguise—opportunities to learn, grow, and improve.

So don't fear them.

It's better to lose and learn something than to win and learn nothing.

Life Lesson 15
Recognize Patterns

A good chess player will be able to look at many different board positions and know exactly what to do, without even having to stop and think about it.

Why? The reason is simple. He has played many games, and been in the same situation many times. He may make different mistakes from one game to the next, but eventually he figures out the right move.

And from that day on he makes the right move every time.

As you improve at chess, you too will come to see board positions the same way. You will learn to recognize patterns - not the shapes created by the setting of the chesspieces, but what their placement actually means to the game.

You will be able to walk up to a game in progress and know which player has a stronger position, what moves were made before you got there, and what moves the players are likely to make next.

And when you play, noticing the patterns that you've seen before will help to make your decisions and judgements faster and easier.

A lot of the game will become automatic. When you make a move, you'll already know what your opponent will do and what you will do after that.

You may have seen chess players who seem to move at lightning speed, and you've wondered how they can think so fast.

The answer is, they're not thinking.

They don't need to anymore. They've played so many games that the moves have become habit. They have paid their dues through years of experience.

At other points in the game they WILL have to stop and think. These are the moments that they're really playing for.

Patterns are everywhere in life. There are patterns in music, in stories, in sports games, in the way two friends talk to one another.

If you pay attention to these patterns, you can learn their rhythm and know how to best fit your actions to the pattern.

And just like the lightning quick chess master, you will know exactly what to do and what to say, blazing along confidently and blowing away everyone around you with what seems like a magical ability.

Life Lesson 16
Use All Your Resources

You start the game with 16 chesspieces. Any one of them might be your ticket to winning. Each of your pawns, Knights, Rooks, Bishops, and the Queen has the chance to be the hero of the day.

Everything depends on how the game unfolds. It would be a mistake to see any of them as unnecessary, or to neglect the opportunities that they can present at the right time and place.

Beginners often underestimate the importance of pawns. But an expert knows that the winner is going to be the one who constantly examines everything he has available, *especially* his pawns, and uses all of his material to maximum effect.

Life works the same way. You have to make the most of what's available to you.

Whatever you want to do, there's a whole world of help out there if you know where and how to look.

Sometimes it's teachers, who show us how to do things and explain how they work. Our friends and family are a gold mine of advice and encouragement. They connect us to an even bigger pool of people who can play a role in helping us achieve our goals.

The Internet is a vast ocean of information where you can find practically anything.

Then there are books, which may be the greatest resource of all. The power and potential in a library is more incredible than you can imagine.

Being able to take maximum advantage of available resources is a skill. Some people are better at it than others.

Chess is a great way to get better. You learn how to work with what is sometimes a limited set of tools.

And once you start forcing checkmates with nothing but your pawns (it can be done!) you will begin to see that success doesn't always go to the richest, smartest, or luckiest person. In fact, often none of those things will be of any help to you at all.

It's much more important to be able to look at what you have available to you, stop, think, and figure out how to make the best use of it.

Life Lesson 17
Work Together

Rooks can only move up and down, side to side; Bishops only in diagonals. But put them together as a team and suddenly the Rook and the Bishop can go anywhere together. They combine their strengths, and pick up the slack for each others weaknesses.

Together they become more powerful than they are on their own.

Your chess results depend on how well you can make your chesspieces work as a group.

Look at them as a group united by a common goal.

If you look at them as individuals working by themselves, you're going to be in trouble.

Try to beat an opponent's entire army with just your Queen—you'll see what I mean. You might make a few captures, but with nobody to help her, she can't make effective attacks or defenses.

The same idea applies anytime you work in a group, even if the group is only two people.

Each member will bring their own individual strengths, abilities, and knowledge to the job.

The more tightly, cooperatively, and efficiently the group works together, the more likely their combined skills will add up, and the more likely that they'll cover each other's weaknesses.

It's not enough to make sure every group member is doing something. Make sure they're all doing what they're best at.

Life will put you into groups over and over again—in school, at work, with friends and family.

One of the rewards of chess is that it will teach you to be a good manager. You'll learn how to divide the work among individuals to get the best results possible.

Watch your games for opportunities to get your chesspieces working as a team. Look for those same kinds of opportunities in your daily life.

Life Lesson 18
Concentrate

Albert Einstein was one of the smartest people who ever lived. His life was full of incredible achievements, and not just because of his high IQ.

The other secret to his success was his remarkable ability to concentrate and stay focused.

Concentration is one of the keys to doing anything well. It will make you sharply aware of the reality of what is happening, right here and right now. It will quiet your feelings, open all your senses, and keep you balanced and relaxed.

You need all of these characteristics to win at chess.

But being able to concentrate requires a lot of training. So work on it every time you play.

The first step is to be patient and calm. You can't think clearly otherwise.

Turn off the chattering of your mind and pay no attention to the world outside the board.

Take a deep breath. For now, let the chess game be the only thing that exists.

Don't rush. Just pay attention to everything that's happening. Let the game reveal itself to you little by little.

Once it's underway, watch your opponent. Take the time to think about what she is doing, and why.

Above all, don't become anxious or impatient. One of the most common mistakes inexperienced players make is to bring out their big pieces too early.

They're playing with their feelings, not purely with their thoughts and observations.

Don't let fear, doubt, suspicion, or anger influence your moves. There may be moments in the game where you feel these things, but shake them off and regain your focus.

Distraction is what keeps us from finishing what we start, from succeeding, or from even attempting new achievements in the first place.

You can't expect to learn perfect concentration overnight, but try to create moments of intense focus as often as you can.

Whether you're trying to win a game of chess or solve a math problem, you'll find yourself getting it done faster and better than you ever thought possible.

Life Lesson 19
Take Risks

Good chess is about making bold moves.

You won't do as well if you just play a safe, cautious game every time. Play unpredictably and aggressively, and most of all creatively.

Always look for that brilliant moment where you can take a daring risk that your opponent won't expect.

You need practice before you see those opportunities, but these are the moves that make chess a blast to play. So don't let them pass you by.

Risk is exciting, and excitement is one of the reasons you're playing in the first place.

One of the most important risks you will learn is sacrificing chess-pieces.

Intentionally giving up material in a game is a scary move. But many times it's exactly what you need, even though it can be hard to accept.

It takes courage and heart to give something up in an attempt to get something greater in return. Many people would rather play it safe, to hold on to what they have, to only go with sure things.

The fact is, I rarely play a chess game where I don't sacrifice at least a few points worth of material.

It could be a few pawns, a Knight, even a Rook if the timing is right.

Sometimes I do it to set a trap, sometimes just to get my pieces where I want them. But what I know for sure is that sacrificing is part of winning.

You have to take big risks in order to get big rewards. You can't win *everything* without giving up *something*.

This doesn't mean that you should be reckless. Good risk-taking means knowing the difference between the smart risks and the unwise ones.

But in the end, the people who achieve the most in the world are the ones who put themselves out there at the right time and take big chances.

Failure is always a possibility. Past failures often keep us from acting when we should.

But sooner or later, a chancey move will lead to victory, and the failures of the past will be forgotten.

♔Life Lesson 20
Down, But Never Out

Your opponent is ahead of you by three pieces. He is in position to attack your King. You feel like it could all end any second.

So what do you do? That's up to you to figure out. But what you DON'T do is quit!

Since I started playing chess, I have seen some amazing comebacks. Players with seemingly no hope of winning at all suddenly roar back from almost nothing to get a miracle victory.

It doesn't just happen in the movies. I've seen it, and I've done it myself.

The players who can do this all have something in common: they *believe* that they can do it.

Then there are players who, in a similar situation, are sure they will lose but continue to play on anyway.

Their focus drains away and they make mistakes, letting themselves fall deeper into the hole until they are defeated.

What these players don't realize is that they didn't lose because they couldn't win. They lost because they stopped looking for a way to win.

If you stumble, it doesn't matter. Stand up, brush yourself off, and move forward. Regain your focus and try again.

Give yourself a chance to make up for your mistake, whatever it is. Don't put any more thought or energy into what you did wrong, and don't convince yourself that you are beaten.

Put it out of your mind, as if it never happened.

Forget about how bad things are right now. Envision them the way you want them to be, and figure out what needs to be done to get there.

Live your life with that attitude.

Giving up is never an option. There's a way to dig yourself out of any hole.

It's never over until checkmate.

Quick Order Form

Fax orders: 831-576-4449. Send a copy of this form

Telephone orders: Call 1-866-7-AUTHOR (That's 866-728-8467) toll free. Have your credit card ready.

Please send me additional copies of *One Move at a Time.* I understand that I may return any of them for a full refund for any reason, no questions asked.

_____ Number of copies at $14.95 each

Please send more FREE information on:
❏ Other Books ❏ Coaching/Consulting
❏ Videos o Speaking/Seminars
❏ Mailing Lists

Name _____

Address _____

City _____ State _____ Zip _____

Telephone (_____) _____

E-mail address _____

Sales Tax: Please add 8.25% for products shipped to California addresses

Shipping by air: U.S.: $5.00 for the first book and $2.00 for each additional. **International:** $12.00 for first book; $7.00 for each additional.

Payment: ❏ Check ❏ Credit Card:
❏Visa ❏Mastercard ❏AMEX ❏Optima ❏Discover

Card number _____

Name on card _____ Exp. Date_____

We give discounts for orders of 10 or more books. Call 866-7-AUTHOR.